ISSUES THAT CONCERN YOU

Career and Technical Education

Cynthia A. Bily, *Book Editor*

GREENHAVEN PRESS
A part of Gale, Cengage Learning

GALE
CENGAGE Learning·

Detroit • New York • San Francisco • New Haven, Conn • Waterville, Maine • London

Elizabeth Des Chenes, *Director, Content Strategy*
Cynthia Sanner, *Publisher*
Douglas Dentino, *Manager, New Product*

Articles in Greenhaven Press anthologies are often edited for length to meet page requirements. In addition, original titles of these works are changed to clearly present the main thesis and to explicitly indicate the author's opinion. Every effort is made to ensure that Greenhaven Press accurately reflects the original intent of the authors. Every effort has been made to trace the owners of copyrighted material.

Cover image © Dmitry Nikolaev/Shutterstock.com.

LIBRARY OF CONGRESS CATALOGING-IN-PUBLICATION DATA

Career and technical education (2013) / Cynthia A. Bily, book editor.
    pages cm. -- (Issues that concern you)
 Includes bibliographical references and index.
 ISBN 978-0-7377-6285-3 (hardcover)
 1. Vocational education. I. Bily, Cynthia A.
 LC1043.C365 2013
 370.113--dc23
                                                          2012051658

Printed in the United States of America
1 2 3 4 5 6 7 17 16 15 14 13

CONTENTS

Introduction   5

1. Career and Technical Education Prepares
   Students for College and Careers   9
   *National Association of State Directors of Career
   Technical Education Consortium*

2. A Four-Year Degree Is the Best Career Preparation   16
   Neil deMause

3. Beyond Home Ec: Vocational Programs
   Are a Good Investment   23
   Andrew P. Kelly

4. Job-Focused Certificates Lead to Well-Paying Jobs   30
   Anthony Carnevale, Stephen J. Rose, and Andrew R. Hanson

5. Today's Workers Need More than Just Job Training   36
   Mary Spilde

6. High School Career and Technical Education
   Takes Time Away from Other Studies   42
   Sarah Butrymowicz

7. High School Programs Must Do a Better Job of
   Preparing Students for College   50
   Arne Duncan

8. Low-Income and Minority Students Are Being
   Squeezed Out of Higher Education   58
   Gary Rhoades

9. Expecting "College for All" Is Misguided   65
   James R. Stone

10. Obtaining a Four-Year Degree Is Not
    Worth the Cost   70
    Sarah Kaufman

11. Career and Technical Programs Can Get
    Dropouts Back on Track   77
    Dorothy Stoneman

12. For-Profit Colleges Are Expensive but Effective   83
    Kevin Carey

13. The Federal Government Should Increase
    Support for Community Colleges   90
    Barack Obama

14. Germany's Career-Focused Education System
    Reduces Unemployment   98
    Edward Lotterman

15. High School Students Should Have More
    Opportunities for Workplace Experience   104
    Dana Goldstein

Appendix

    What You Should Know About Career and
    Technical Education   111

    What You Should Do About Career and
    Technical Education   116

Organizations to Contact   119

Bibliography   125

Index   128

Picture Credits   134

"Over the past five years, most manufacturers have redesigned and streamlined their production lines while implementing more process automation. In short, as the industry has changed, the nature of work that it requires is changing as well. It's happening fast, and manufacturers will continue to expect more from their employees."

—Manufacturing Institute, 2012

After years of prosperity, the US economy began to weaken severely in 2008. A combination of a sudden drop in the value of people's homes and complicated mistakes made by financial organizations took the country into a recession, and many of those hurt in the decline were middle-class workers. As homes and investments lost their value, businesses closed, and many people lost their jobs. According to the US Bureau of Labor Statistics, the national unemployment rate was 5.0 percent in January 2008; by January 2010 it was 9.7 percent, meaning that almost one in ten of those who were able to work and were actively looking for work could not find jobs.

Since early 2010 the economy has gradually gotten stronger, new jobs have been created, and many people are back to work; however, another trend has shaped the nature of many of these new jobs: Over several decades, new technology has changed how many tasks in manufacturing, health care, agriculture, and other industries are performed. In the past, manufacturers might hire hundreds of people without much education or training to do repetitive tasks on an assembly line, but today's manufacturing plants have robots to do the repetitive work and highly trained employees to operate the robots, using computers. This has led to a strange phenomenon: While there are many people looking for work, many industries say that they cannot find enough workers with the proper training to fill open positions, and by mid-2012 the Manufacturing Institute

Career and technical education programs include engineering, health care/biomedical, renewable energy, hospitality, nanotechnology, law enforcement, information technology, and other fields.

reported that there were a half million positions available in manufacturing.

This mismatch between available workers and available jobs is commonly attributed to what is called a "skills gap." It points back to the changing nature of work in the twenty-first century, as more tasks that used to be done by hand are now done by machine and as new industries in information technology, communication, and medical technology have grown. This changing landscape offers exciting opportunities for students who are still in school and thinking about their future careers—if they get the right kinds of education and training. What kind of training will they need? Kevin P. Reilly asked that question in an October 13, 2012, column for the *Milwaukee Journal Sentinel:* "Today's students will likely spend most of their working lifetimes in jobs, organizations and industries that do not yet exist. How should we prepare students now to make their livelihood in companies not yet invented?"

For many students, the answer lies in career and technical education (CTE), the twenty-first-century version of what used to be called vocational and technical education, or vo-tech. But while the old vo-tech programs, particularly in high schools, sometimes channeled weak or disengaged students away from academic programs and into labor, the new CTE programs provide a solid education based on a combination of traditional academics and hands-on, career-focused courses, helping students of all abilities and interests acquire what are commonly called twenty-first-century skills. As explained in the 2010 report *Up to the Challenge: The Role of Career and Technical Education and 21st Century Skills in College and Career Readiness*, "College and career readiness requires both knowledge and skills. It's time to abandon the false dichotomy between knowledge and skills. Knowledge is necessary, but not sufficient, for success today. Students need skills to be able to apply their knowledge and continue learning." Career and technical education is found in high schools, public and private colleges, technical schools, and even employer training programs. Students who complete certificates or associate's degrees through these programs are often ready to take on rewarding and well-paying jobs in a variety of fields.

The changing landscape of educational demands and opportunities in the twenty-first century—and how students can best navigate this landscape—are addressed by the authors of the viewpoints in *Issues That Concern You: Career and Technical Education*. In addition, the volume contains several appendixes to help the reader understand and explore the topic, including a thorough bibliography and a list of organizations to contact for further information. The appendix titled "What You Should Know About Career and Technical Education" offers facts about twenty-first-century careers and the training needed to perform these jobs, as well as a sampling of public opinion about career and technical education. The appendix "What You Should Do About Career and Technical Education" offers tips for young people interested in finding a career path that suits their skills and interests and in finding the right place to get more training and education after high school. With all these features, *Issues That Concern You: Career and Technical Education* provides an excellent resource for everyone interested in this issue.

ONE

Career and Technical Education Prepares Students for College and Careers

National Association of State Directors of Career Technical Education Consortium

> In the following viewpoint the authors describe a new vision for career technical education (CTE). Current CTE programs, they explain, grew out of twentieth-century vocational and technical programs, but there is an important difference: Whereas in the past many educators believed that preparing for a career and preparing for college were widely separate paths, the modern workforce demands workers with the same academic skills—including communication and critical thinking—that are developed by students pursuing four-year and graduate degrees. In order for the United States to maintain a competitive advantage over other nations and emerge from economic downturns, the viewpoint argues, CTE programs must work with academic and business leaders to prepare students to be skilled, adaptable, lifelong learners.
>
> The National Association of State Directors of Career Technical Education Consortium represents state and territorial heads of secondary, postsecondary, and adult career technical education across the United States.

The United States has long held its leading economic status in the world. Propelled by innovation, the competitive character of capitalism, and the spirit of entrepreneurship, our nation thrived as a power house setting both the standards and pace for the world economy. On the heels of national fiscal crises, a flattening globe, and the challenges and opportunities brought on by technology, we must now take a hard look at how our workforce is prepared if the United States is to retain its leadership position in the dynamic global economy.

In the early 1900s, vocational education emerged in response to the burgeoning industrial era. Designed to train individuals with job-specific skills, vocational education helped drive our nation's economic engine throughout the 20th century. Today, vocational education is called career technical education (CTE). To be clear—CTE is not a new label for the same system. While CTE is built upon the rich history and tradition of vocational education, it has adapted to meet the dynamic demands of the global economy. CTE programs at the secondary, postsecondary and adult levels prepare individuals for a wide range of careers such as health care/bio-medical, renewable energy, hospitality, nanotechnology, engineering, logistics, law enforcement, and information technology. As such, CTE reflects the modern workplace. And since the majority of careers require a postsecondary credential, high-quality CTE programs incorporate rigorous academic and technical standards, as well as critical workplace skills such as problem solving, communication and teamwork, to ensure career and college success for its students.

Hence, CTE has a positive impact on student achievement and transitions. The programs help students find their passion, bolster their confidence and empower them to succeed. Because CTE demonstrates a positive return on investment, CTE is a trusted, long-standing partner with the employer community. And since CTE programs can be found in rural, suburban and urban communities in every state in our nation, CTE has the capacity and infrastructure to be the vehicle to prepare students of all ages to be successful in this ever-changing, world marketplace. While many CTE programs have evolved in the ways noted above, not all have. We have made much progress but we can and must go further. Excellence in all of our programs is essential.

Transform: A Reinvention

The forecasted needs of the 21st century, the pace of technological change, demographics, the challenges of student engagement and achievement, and growing global competition have created an urgency to evaluate the trajectory and role of CTE in the United States. In keeping with our leadership role and responsibility, the National Association of State Directors of Career Technical Education Consortium puts forth this bold vision intended to guide CTE's role in our nation's educational, workforce and economic advancement and success.

Students at a Colorado career and technical education center mix paints as part of their training in auto-body repair.

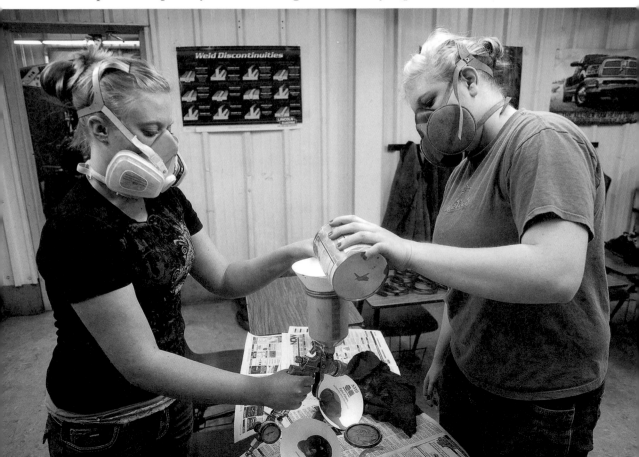

The five principles below collectively form our vision for CTE. The principles are interdependent and should not be considered in isolation. This vision charts a progressive, challenging agenda that seeks to ensure that CTE's contributions and potential are fully realized.

By meeting the current needs and anticipating the future demands of the economy, CTE is critical to our nation's economic success. CTE is a leader in building collaborative connections among education, economic development, and workforce development to ensure alignment of policies and program delivery. The programs are flexible in how and when they are delivered, and are innovative and quick to respond to employer needs. Standards incorporated in the programs are rigorous, blended academic and technical content, and internationally benchmarked. And students of all ages—youth to adult—who enroll in these programs are prepared as global citizens with an innovative and entrepreneurial spirit and who are boundless in their ideas and endeavors to stimulate positive economic change. . . .

CTE aligns its programmatic offerings to current, emerging and projected labor market needs. Therefore, partnership with business and industry is absolutely essential to our success. Drawing our curricula, standards and organizing principles from the workplace, employers are critical partners in the design and delivery of CTE programs. . . .

The false dichotomy of preparation for work or college is no longer relevant. The global economy places a premium on skills acquisition and innovation. Therefore, all workers must be lifelong learners who continue to cultivate and grow their knowledge and skills through further education. CTE programs prepare students to be successful by providing adaptable skills and knowledge, thereby ensuring flexibility to transition careers as interests change, opportunities emerge and the economy transforms. To document competency of these knowledge and skills, valid and reliable assessments that result in nationally recognized and portable credentials are necessary.

To achieve our vision, ongoing transformation in the content and delivery of CTE programs is necessary. Programs of study aligned to The National Career Clusters framework [a nationally recognized definition of college and career readiness] are the means to accomplish this goal and should be the method of delivery of all of CTE. A rigorous and comprehensive program of study, delivered by qualified instructors, is a structured sequence of academic and CTE courses that leads to a postsecondary-level credential. In a program of study, the standards, curriculum, and assessments are aligned, thereby ensuring coordination and seamless delivery of instruction and transitions for students. Students are given opportunities to explore myriad career possibilities and have access to comprehensive career planning that empowers them to plan and prepare for a lifetime of career and educational choices. Relevant work-based learning opportunities, and leadership development offered through career technical student organizations (CTSOs), are incorporated into the program of study. . . .

CTE embraces the critical importance of accountability and data-driven decisions. CTE's performance must be measured by appropriate indicators that accurately reflect programmatic outcomes. Data is used to drive decisions on resources and programs, thus ensuring programs are aligned to the economy's needs and resources are directed toward areas of highest need. Further, data demonstrates CTE's positive impact through return on investment measured by fiscal returns or savings for government and employers, favorable societal impact, career benefits for individuals and a positive impact on regional, state or national economies. . . .

Lead: A Call to Action

Our nation is at a critical juncture as competition in the global economy intensifies. We believe our nation's economic vitality hinges on our commitment to invest in and ensure the preparedness, efficiency, innovation, creativity and productivity of the U.S. workforce.

CTE also has reached a critical juncture. Success in this global economic environment demands a different type of workforce. If CTE is to have a role in successfully preparing this workforce, we must look at program content, how we deliver our programs,

"High Need" for Applied Skills

The percentage of employers reporting a "high need" for training programs in these twenty-first-century job skills.

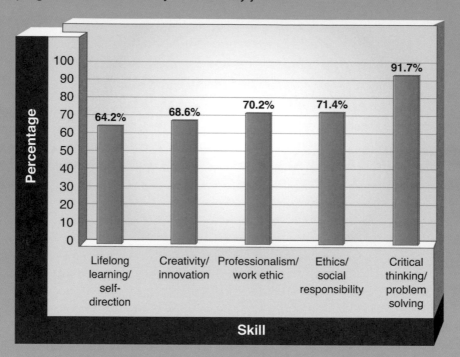

Taken from: The Conference Board, Corporate Voices for Working Families, American Society for Training & Development, and The Society for Human Resource Management. *The Ill-Prepared US Workforce: Exploring the Challenges of Employer-Provided Readiness Training*, 2009.

and let go of what no longer works. We will strive to create only programs of excellence. We must be willing to take the bold steps necessary to jumpstart dramatic change in our nation's education and workforce preparation systems. The dichotomous silos of academics versus CTE must be eliminated and their supporting infrastructures must be re-imagined to meet the needs of the economy. As the lines of economies blur, so too must the lines that currently separate CTE and academic education.

As we look to the future, imagine an education and workforce system that rewards innovation, and synergistically and cohesively supports different learning styles, equally values different interests and talents, nimbly adapts and responds to technology and workplace needs, and prepares all students for career success through multiple pathways. This is our vision for the future of CTE. Bold leadership and actions will be necessary to realize this vision. We will provide the leadership to ensure our vision is achieved.

TWO

A Four-Year Degree Is the Best Career Preparation

Neil deMause

In the following viewpoint Neil deMause argues that a four-year college degree is well worth its cost. Not every college and not every academic major leads to the highest return, he acknowledges, and it will take many students years to pay back their student loans and realize the full financial benefits of their degrees. But although the current economic situation makes the future appear shaky even for graduates, ten years after graduation those with degrees will be in a much better situation than those who did not attend college, he concludes.

A journalist, deMause writes for books, magazines, and newspapers.

In a few weeks, close to 2 million students will head off to college, ready to spend four years studying, socializing, and accumulating the kind of debt load that would make the Greek government blush. With both tuitions and debt loads on the rise—both are now at record highs—college-bound seniors and their check-writing parents will be excused for wondering: Is all this time and money worth it? Not worth it in terms of intangibles like lifelong friends made, ineffable truths revealed, or brain cells killed by things that will cause you trouble at your later Senate confirmation hearings, but worth it in a cold, hard economic sense: If you could buy a diploma on eBay, what would be a reasonable price to pay for it?

Fortunately, there are plenty of studies out there giving answers to the question of what a college degree is worth. In fact, you can find just about any answer you like: Want to learn that a diploma will boost your lifetime earnings by about $700,000? The Census Bureau's American Community Survey has you covered. That putting money into a diploma returns more than twice what you'd get by putting it into the stock market? The Brookings Institution's Hamilton Project has done that calculation. That 40 percent of graduates' first jobs out of college don't even require a four-year degree? Hello, Rutgers Center for Workforce Development!

The basic principle, at least, is easy to calculate: Take the population of college graduates and compare their lifetime earnings to those of the sheepskin deprived. Convert to present dollars. Subtract the cost of a college diploma. Voilà! That's the added value of your four years spent toiling beneath ivory towers.

There are, however, several complications that make the calculus less certain. Because not everyone attends the same school or graduates with the same major, "average" earnings aren't going to mean much if you're weighing, say, a private liberal arts school versus community college. People who go to college are also, well, the kind of people who go to college, which leaves open the question of whether it's the degree producing those increased earnings or their own inherent braininess. And, of course, not everyone who starts college finishes—which as the Brookings study notes, can be a situation "resulting in educational costs but not leading to a degree."

The result is the blind-men-and-the-elephant mess [truths stemming from different perspectives] that largely typifies college-earnings studies and massively confuses prospective students and their parents. As Sandy Baum, author of two studies of graduate earnings for the College Board, says: "People really like simple answers. And it's just not that simple."

After a review of the literature and some follow-up calls to those responsible, however, some conclusions are possible:

On average, most college graduates earn back enough to pay off their student expenses within a decade or so. Two studies by Baum found that graduates with a bachelor's and no further schooling—or as the earnings literature calls it a bit too on point, a "terminal bachelor's"—are on average able to repay their college tuition and loans, living expenses, and lost income from skipping four years of work by the time they turn 33. Private-college graduates spend more on their degrees, Baum says, but as they also have slightly higher earning power than their public-college counterparts, they still on the average earn back their college costs before age 40.

Brookings's Hamilton Project took the same numbers and crunched them differently, establishing the total cost of a college degree (including tuition, fees, board, and the lost income from spending four years lugging books for free instead of getting paid to sling French fries) at $102,000 and then estimating whether an 18-year-old would be better off spending that much on a college education or just buying stocks. Their conclusion: Investing in college results in an average return of 15.2 percent a year, "more than double the average return to stock market investments since 1950 and more than five times the returns to corporate bonds, gold, long-term government bonds, or home ownership. From any investment perspective, college is a great deal."

If everybody followed this advice, it might not be true anymore. "If you look at young college graduates, the wages they earn now are substantially below what it was in the year 2000," says Lawrence Mishel, director of the D.C.-based Economic Policy Institute [EPI], which has extensively studied relative earnings for differing educational levels. "If we flood the market with more college graduates, this trend will only be exacerbated."

This already happened once before, Mishel notes: In the 1970s, when young American men fleeing the draft emerged with degrees in unprecedented numbers, it led the "education premium" for increased earnings from a college degree to plunge by more than 20 percent.

Education Pays

According to the US Department of Labor, higher education leads to higher earnings and lower unemployment rates.

Unemployment Rate in 2011 (in Percentages)

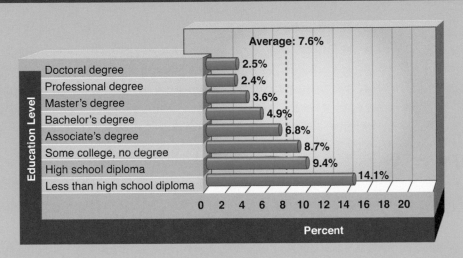

Average: 7.6%

Education Level	Percent
Doctoral degree	2.5%
Professional degree	2.4%
Master's degree	3.6%
Bachelor's degree	4.9%
Associate's degree	6.8%
Some college, no degree	8.7%
High school diploma	9.4%
Less than high school diploma	14.1%

Median Weekly Earnings in 2011 (in Dollars Earned)

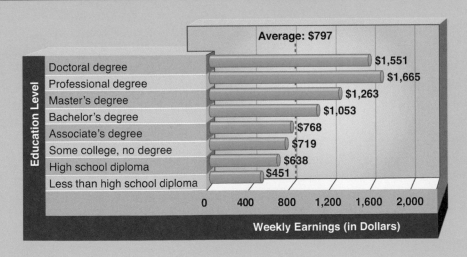

Average: $797

Education Level	Weekly Earnings (in Dollars)
Doctoral degree	$1,551
Professional degree	$1,665
Master's degree	$1,263
Bachelor's degree	$1,053
Associate's degree	$768
Some college, no degree	$719
High school diploma	$638
Less than high school diploma	$451

Taken from: US Department of Labor, Bureau of Labor Statistics, last updated March 23, 2012. www.bls.gov.

"We now have a third of the people with a college degree or more. If in 2020, instead of 33 percent, we had 43 percent, do we think there would be jobs requiring a college degree for everybody who had a college degree? The answer would be no."

A college degree is more valuable to those who are on the bubble of getting in. "The return's not the same to everybody," Baum says, noting that people who are not currently going to college, if they enrolled, wouldn't likely end up the highest earners because they wouldn't be the top students. "But some studies show that they get the biggest benefit because they're really in bad shape if they don't go to college." In other words, if you were writing code in sixth grade like [Facebook founder] Mark Zuckerberg, dropping out of Harvard is likely a more viable career option than if you'll need that diploma to get through a recruiter's door.

Studies have shown that college graduates who have earned a bachelor's degree are, on average, able to repay their college loans by the age of thirty-three.

Majors matter. "What's It Worth? The Economic Value of College Majors," a 2011 study by Georgetown University's Center on Education and the Workforce, noted that the average graduate with a petroleum-engineering degree earns four times as much as the average counseling psychology major. Of the 10 most popular majors, computer science tops the earnings list with a $75,000 median salary; at the bottom is elementary education, at $40,000.

"When you sign up for your major, they ought to give you a little pamphlet that tells you what happened to people over in that major. I think that given the price of these things, you ought to get a prospectus when you buy in," says Anthony Carnevale, the Georgetown study's lead author. "But most young people go to college in order to graduate. They do what interests them—they don't think at all about how it relates to a career."

What school you go to matters, but only sometimes. "The selective schools are the best places to get a liberal arts degree, and the best places to go if you want to get a graduate degree," Carnevale says. "If you go to Harvard to become a schoolteacher, you won't make any more than someone who went to UDC [University of the District of Columbia, a public school] in Washington." The main advantage of going to an expensive, selective, high-ranking school, say researchers: You have a much higher chance of graduating in four years, though whether that's a function of how great the schools are or of how great you are for being accepted there is an open question.

Past returns are no guarantee of future performance. According to EPI's figures, which control for age, gender, and race, the value of a college diploma versus a high school certificate rose steadily through the '80s and '90s—but since then, Mishel says, "It's grown bupkes."

That's overstating things just a bit, as the education premium actually inched upwards by a percentage point or two from 2001 to 2011, per EPI's numbers. Still, even these modest gains are less because the average college graduate is making tons of money—their earnings actually fell over that decade—than because the earning power of high school graduates has been declining for decades, especially for men. Which leads us to—

If college is no sure thing, not going to college is even worse. Just about all the studies agree on one thing: No matter how dicey things look for college graduates, things are so dismal right now for people with only high school diplomas, you better get into whatever lifeboat you can, even if it leaves you $100,000 in debt.

"The underbelly of all of this," says Hamilton Project director Michael Greenstone, "is this differential between college and no college is a function of two things: One is the level of how much you get paid for going to college. But it's also a function of what you get paid for only having a high school credential." And that has plummeted, especially for men: According to figures compiled by Brookings, while the inflation-adjusted median earnings of full-time male workers with college degrees dipped 2 percent from 1969 to 2009, for those with high school diplomas, it sunk 26 percent.

The culprit is easy to pinpoint: As manufacturing jobs have fled overseas, the few low-skill jobs that remain in the U.S. increasingly sport developing-nation wages. "The decline in earnings for people with less than college in real terms is really astonishing over the last 30 or 40 years," Greenstone says. "It's just very challenging to have a middle-class lifestyle without having a college degree or more."

It certainly puts those inevitable tales of overeducated baristas in a different light when you consider all the undereducated baristas who are now stuck in the unemployment lines. If you graduate from college today, Baum acknowledges, "you might work at Starbucks for a year or two until the economy recovers." But even if recent college graduates are facing crappier work prospects than their older siblings, she predicts, "they're going to be fine in 10 years. Whereas the people who just graduated high school? They're not going to be so fine."

THREE

Beyond Home Ec: Vocational Programs Are a Good Investment

Andrew P. Kelly

In the following viewpoint Andrew P. Kelly argues that the American education system has failed young people by encouraging them to go to college whether or not they can afford it and by directing them to academic programs that do not lead to good jobs. In the next decade, he contends, millions of new jobs will become available to workers with associate's degrees or occupational certificates rather than four-year degrees. He concludes that federal funding and public school education should be directed more toward career and technical education programs in high school and beyond.

Kelly is a research fellow at the American Enterprise Institute, a public policy think tank in Washington, DC.

The Occupy Wall Street protests have reintroduced a recurring character in our national economic drama: the struggling young college graduate. Every time the economy goes south, we hear from the Harvard-educated bartender, the taxi driver with a master's degree in art history, or the philosophy major who's moved back in with his parents, shipping out résumé after fruitless résumé. As Ezra Klein recounts in the *Washington Post*, many of the Occupy Wall Street protesters cite their college loans as a source of their grievances: "College debt represents a special sort of betrayal. We told you that the way to get ahead in America was to get educated. You did it. And now you find yourself in the same place, but buried under debt. You were lied to."

Lost in this rhetoric is any suggestion that it is the education system—the schools that charged all that money and then provided little by way of marketable skills in return—that let these young people down. There's plenty of criticism for corporations that aren't hiring and banks that are calling to collect their loans, but don't the institutions that failed to prepare students for the world of work deserve part of the blame? Some of these talented people would no doubt have been better served by an education more directly tied to the jobs they so desperately need.

Four-year colleges and universities are reluctant to see the education they provide as "occupational." High schools are often rated according to how many of their students go off to a four-year college, not how many find success in the labor market out of high school or move on to an occupational program at a community college. Overlaying all of this is an intense sensitivity to charges that disadvantaged students are being pushed onto educational pathways that do not lead to a bachelor's degree.

But employment projections suggest that prioritizing only bachelor's-degree production is a mistake. The Georgetown Center for Education and the Workforce projects that U.S. employers will have 47 million job openings between 2010 and 2018, 30 million of which will require some post-secondary education. Fourteen million of these positions will require an associate's degree or a vocational certificate rather than a bachelor's degree—the so-called middle-skill jobs such as electrician, health-care aide, and construction manager. Based on these projections, the Georgetown researchers estimate that by 2025, the U.S. will require 4 million additional occupational certificates and 1 million more associate's degrees to meet employer demand.

Surveys of employers routinely uncover a mismatch between what they need from their employees and what prospective hires

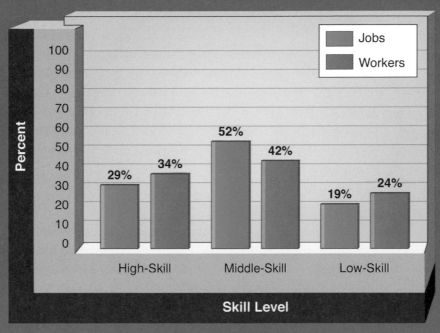

US Jobs and Workers, by Skill Level

According to the US Department of Labor, the number of so-called middle-skills jobs available in the United States is greater than the number of workers who are qualified to fill them.

Taken from: Armand Biroonak. "Job Creation? Not Without Worker Training." Institute for America's Future, January 28, 2010. http://institute.ourfuture.org.

of all educational backgrounds bring to the table. A 2006 survey of employers by the Conference Board found that 42 percent of respondents considered the overall preparation of recent high-school graduates for entry-level jobs "deficient." A similar survey by the Association of American Colleges and Universities reported that 63 percent of employers believe recent college graduates lack the skills necessary for success in the global economy.

For their part, students wish that their high-school and college courses were more closely tied to the world of work. The 2009 High School Survey of Student Engagement revealed that

40 percent of high-school students were bored in school because the curriculum was not relevant to the real world. Just 26 percent thought that high school provided skills necessary for work after graduation.

All signs suggest it's time to rethink our approach to vocational education, now called "career and technical education" or CTE, and make it a central piece of our economic recovery.

The federal government has been funding vocational-education programs since World War I, almost 50 years before the Elementary and Secondary Education Act of 1965 got the feds involved in the remainder of pre-college education. Policymakers sought to keep vocational education separate from traditional academics by placing restrictions on which courses and teachers were eligible to receive federal dollars: Teachers of academic disciplines were not eligible to receive federal funds, and there were limits on the number of academic credits that vocational students could take.

Though originally designed to prevent schools from using federal funds for non-vocational training, this firewall between the vocational and the academic ensured that CTE would be marginalized for much of the following century. Recent spending reflects this marginalization; in 2008, for every dollar that the feds spent on elementary and secondary education, vocational-education programs got about one cent. That same year, the states spent an average of less than $20 per student on vocational education, compared with $94 per student on transportation and $340 per student on special education.

Earlier this year, Education Secretary Arne Duncan tersely summed up the place of vocational education in the country's educational hierarchy: "For far too long, CTE has been the neglected stepchild of education reform. That neglect has to stop." But President Obama's 2012 budget promises more of the same, recommending a 20 percent cut to federal CTE programs at the same time that it calls for increasing overall education spending by 11 percent.

Policymakers should instead learn from an array of career-education programs that have sprouted up in high schools, technical colleges, and for-profit institutions around the country. These programs bear little resemblance to the home-ec and woodshop classes of yesteryear. Most are focused on preparing students for such growing industries as health care, information technology, and engineering. Most important, they are closely linked to local employers.

At the high-school level, school districts have experimented with "career academies" for 30 years, often to great effect. Career academies are schools-within-schools; students apply to an industry-focused academy, and their coursework is tailored to teach the skills and knowledge needed to be successful in the industry. The academies also partner with local employers to provide students with on-the-job experience. An eight-year evaluation of nine urban career academies found that academy graduates out-earned non-academy students by more than $2,000 per year (or $16,700 over the eight-year period), and that the advantage was particularly pronounced among young men, who earned an average of $3,700 more per year than their peers.

For post-secondary students, evidence is mounting that the payoff for occupational-certificate programs of at least one year can be quite large—often outweighing the benefits of an associate or bachelor's degree. Nationally, the Georgetown Center for Education and the Workforce estimates that 43 percent of workers with occupational certificates and licenses out-earned associate-degree holders, and 27 percent had higher earnings than bachelor's-degree recipients.

Evidence from Florida reveals a similar pattern: Graduates with a post-secondary certificate from a Florida community college earned $2,500 more per year than bachelor's-degree recipients from the state's four-year colleges. Certificates in health care, nursing, and information technology tend to post the strongest returns, and almost 45 percent of the certificates awarded in 2007–08 were in health care and related fields.

These certificate programs also make more efficient use of public dollars. Completion rates for certificate programs are often quite high—typically between 65 and 75 percent of students finish and attain the credential—which helps keep their cost per

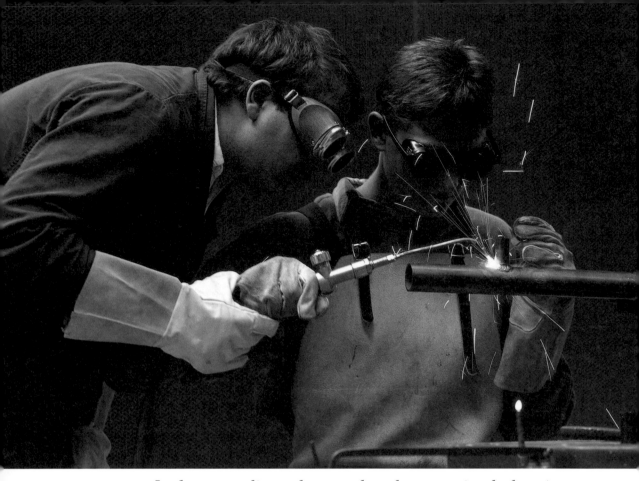

In the past, policy makers sought to keep vocational education separate from traditional academics by placing restrictions on which courses were federally subsidized, with the result that vocational training received far less support than traditional academics.

completion lower than that of degree programs with higher rates of attrition. The contrast is evident in Tennessee, where 27 state-run technology centers that award occupational certificates have had an average completion rate of about 70 percent over the last five years. At the state's 13 community colleges, completion rates hover around 15 to 20 percent. An analysis by Complete College America found that the state paid about $7,500 per completion at the tech centers in 2008, compared with just over $26,000 per degree at the community colleges. And it's not that the tech centers are just churning graduates through low-quality programs: The job-placement rate for tech-center graduates (83 percent) is comparable to the rate for Tennessee's community-college graduates (91 percent).

The point is not that every student should follow a career-academy or tech-center model. Every approach has its limits, and traditional associate or bachelor's programs will continue to be right for many students. But it should not be a surprise that innovative CTE programs have proven successful. They teach practical, marketable skills and are tightly linked to employer demand in high-growth industries. Many of them feature a heavy dose of on-the-job training and apprenticeships that introduce students to local employers and provide them with the personal relationships that often underlie the labor market.

The recession has pinned education policy in a tough spot: Our schools must both produce more skilled workers and do so as efficiently as possible. Innovative models of career and technical education could go a long way toward threading this needle. With some initiative and imagination, policymakers and leaders in the private sector can transform CTE from an educational backwater into an engine of our economic recovery.

FOUR

Job-Focused Certificates Lead to Well-Paying Jobs

Anthony P. Carnevale, Stephen J. Rose, and Andrew R. Hanson

> In the following viewpoint Anthony P. Carnevale, Stephen J. Rose, and Andrew R. Hanson argue that certificate programs run by business, vocational, trade, and technical schools can offer certificate holders an important boost in their skills and earning power. Although the programs are uneven in quality, they note, the best programs can lead to good jobs in much less time than it takes to earn a traditional associate's or bachelor's degree and give many students the skills and confidence to go on to complete degree programs. In a troubled economy and an ever-changing work environment, they conclude, certificates can help make a variety of learners more employable.
>
> Carnevale is the director, Rose an economist, and Hanson a research analyst at the Georgetown University Center on Education and the Workforce.

In America, the postsecondary certificate has become a cost-effective tool for increasing postsecondary educational attainment and gainful employment. Certificates are a homegrown

American invention and are expanding rapidly in response to a wide range of educational and labor market demands.

Certificates vary widely in their benefits, but have the capacity to raise the country's global educational standing by both encouraging further education and degree completion as well as by providing gainful employment. Two out of every three workers who have a certificate and a college degree earned the certificate first, an indication that certificates can serve as a stepping stone on the way to a college degree.

Even if only certificates with demonstrated value were included among America's postsecondary credentials, the United States would move from 15th to 10th in postsecondary completions among Organization for Economic Cooperation and Development (OECD) countries for those 25- to 34-years-old. Despite the growing importance of certificates—one million are awarded each year—only one of the major government socioeconomic surveys has information on certificate holding. Consequently, there are very few studies or reports focused on this education/training option.

Bite-Sized Awards with Clear Value

Certificates tend to be occupationally focused and rely on training in specific fields as opposed to the broader general education approach of two- and four-year degrees. There is wide variation in the economic returns to certificates based on field of study, sex, and ability to get a job related to one's training. At a time when 36 million American workers who attended college did not complete a degree, certificates are piecemeal, attainable, bite-sized educational awards that can add substantially to postsecondary completion.

The extraordinary growth in certificates has coincided with increased public scrutiny of the economic value of postsecondary gainful employment programs, especially those offered by for-profit colleges. Thus far, the result has been an expansion in public regulation intended to make certain that postsecondary programs supported by public grants and federally subsidized loans lead to gainful employment.

Certificates are not currently counted in some metrics as the country pushes toward greater postsecondary attainment. But many certificates do count when it comes to economic value. For example, even if we only counted certificates with clear and demonstrable economic value over high school diplomas, the postsecondary attainment rate among American workers would increase by roughly five percentage points from 41 percent to 46 percent.

Low-Hanging Fruit

Even more high school graduates, particularly those from low-income families, have the academic potential to complete certificates but currently are not doing so. Other high school graduates are completing certificate programs, but working outside their field of study or in low-paying fields. These groups represent "low-hanging fruit" [i.e., easily gained rewards] that would move us beyond 46 percent toward the national goal of 60 percent of the workforce with a postsecondary credential.

Certificates with economic value are cost-effective, partly because they are the quickest education and job training awards offered by American higher education. Certificates almost always take less than two years to complete, and more than half take less than one year. They also often pay off more than two-year degrees and sometimes pay off more than four-year degrees.

These bite-sized educational awards also provide the on-ramp to college education and middle-class jobs for low-income, minority and immigrant Americans who are often the first in their families to attend college. For incumbent workers, certificates can be the most effective way to catch up, keep up and get ahead in their chosen field. For the unemployed and underemployed, certificates can offer a jumpstart in the labor market. . . .

Certificates and Lifelong Learning

In an economy in which the lockstep march from school to work has been replaced by lifelong learning, certificates provide flexible

Apprentice certificate programs run by business, vocational trades, and technical schools can give participants an important boost to their skills and earning power and can lead to good jobs in less time than it takes to earn an associate's or bachelor's degree.

learning modules that fit wherever necessary in an increasingly nonlinear education and training system. The lifelong value of certificates is evident in the age distribution of certificate earners. While 66 percent of certificate holders earn their certificates before age 30, 18 percent are in their 30s and 16 percent are 40 or older.

Certificates count when it comes to leveraging gainful employment in a variety of ways. On average, certificate holders earn 20 percent more than high school–educated workers—about $240,000 over a high school diploma in lifetime earnings. More than 60 percent of certificates have a clearly demonstrated economic payoff over high school diplomas—i.e., earnings 10 percent higher than the median high school graduate. Moreover, even when certificates don't provide much of an earnings boost, they can make individuals more employable, giving them access to valuable learning on the job. . . .

In an American economy where the advancement of technology and globalization means that a high school diploma alone is no longer able to provide family-sustaining earnings to many, certificates represent one piece of a multi-pronged solution on the

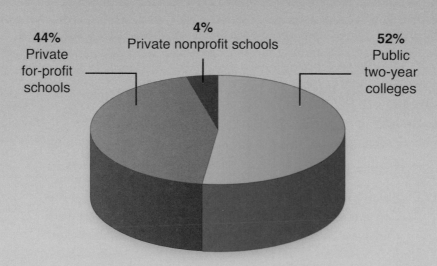

Who Awards Certificates?

44%
Private for-profit schools

4%
Private nonprofit schools

52%
Public two-year colleges

Data source: Integrated Postsecondary Education Data System (IPEDS)

Taken from: Anthony P. Carnevale, Stephen J. Rose, and Andrew R. Hanson. *Certificates: Gateway to Gainful Employment and College Degrees.* Georgetown University Center on Education and the Workforce, June 2012. www9.georgetown.edu.

road to a workforce with 60 percent postsecondary attainment. Though certificates currently aren't counted in many measures of postsecondary attainment, often they provide the outcomes that degree-seeking students are looking for: gainful employment. Certificates can also serve as the first rung on the ladder to a college degree or as training for workers with degrees engaged in the process of lifelong learning and career advancement. The rapid growth of certificates over the past 30 years is a promising signal that students and institutions are recognizing the value of certificates at an increasing rate.

Today, policymakers do have a role: to ensure that all parties involved know, to the greatest extent possible, that the value of the programs they are funding are transparent for all to see. Certificate programs are successful if they promote either: (1) gainful employment and long-term job and income security or (2) the pursuit of a higher-level credential, typically a college degree. If they are successful in these two areas, certificate programs will ensure that students considering them will be able to make informed choices about what to study and where to study it, with reasonable expectations about their prospects after graduation.

FIVE

Today's Workers Need More than Just Job Training

Mary Spilde

In the following viewpoint Mary Spilde speaks for the value of a broad, or "liberal," education—an education that includes science, culture, and society—for all students, not just for students in four-year college degree programs. Even students working toward technical certificates and degrees will need to communicate through writing and speaking, to solve problems, and to understand how what they are doing affects and is affected by the wider world, she argues. Employers demand a broadly educated workforce, she concludes, and community colleges should push all of their students toward a liberal education.

Spilde is president of Lane Community College in Oregon and a board member of the Association of American Colleges and Universities.

I was very proud earlier this year [2010] to stand with my fellow community college leaders pledging to increase college student completion rates by 50 percent over the next decade. We knew then and know now, however, that even as we work diligently to remove barriers to progression and completion, we must also ensure that all students actually leave with the skills and knowledge they need to succeed in today's world.

Today's college students, in fact, need to complete their programs with field-specific skills and the broad outcomes of a liberal education.

Few people think of community college students when they hear the words "liberal education." This is unfortunate, given how important the outcomes of an engaged, 21st century liberal education are in today's world—not just for the privileged students attending elite liberal arts colleges, but for all students, regardless of where they start or finish their educational journeys.

What the general public may not know is that nearly all community colleges, including my own, Lane Community College (Lane) in Oregon, seek to provide a solid grounding in liberal education to all students, including those students pursuing technical degrees. Without this grounding, students with these degrees would not be well positioned to succeed over the long term as they navigate their way through a constantly churning and challenging economic environment.

Tools for Global Citizenship

This fall, Lane began implementing a new strategic plan. Central to this plan is a commitment to expanding a practical liberal education model throughout our programs and services. We are committed to empowering our students to become global citizens by providing them with liberal education outcomes—things like the ability to effectively communicate orally and in writing, the ability to think critically and to problem-solve, to understand the global context of their field, and the ability to understand the substantive issues at stake in today's public policy debates and exercise responsibility in their roles as citizens.

It is deeply gratifying that, while the term "liberal education" may not be generally associated with the work of community colleges, the outcomes of a liberal education are embraced within the community college movement.

Employers Identify "Essential Learning Outcomes"

In a 2010 survey commissioned by the Association of American Colleges and Universities, employers said that they want colleges to "place more emphasis" on students' knowledge of human cultures and the physical and natural world.

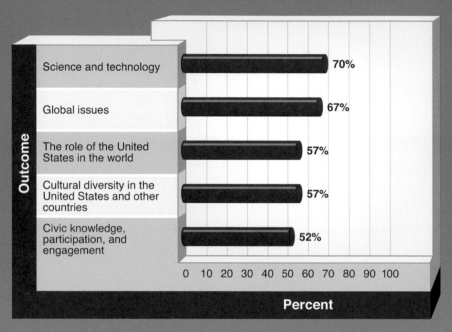

Taken from: *Raising the Bar: Employers' Views on College Learning in the Wake of the Economic Downturn*, survey conducted for AAC&U by Hart Research Associates, 2010. www.aacu.org.

Employers of our graduates are also desperate to find more workers with the skills and abilities developed through a liberal education. In a recent forum in our state, sponsored as part of the Association of American Colleges and Universities' (AAC&U) Liberal Education and America's Promise (LEAP) initiative—of which Lane is an active participant—Steven Pratt, then chair of the Oregon Business Council and an influential CEO [chief executive officer] of ESCO Corp., noted that his company "lives and dies on (its) ability to innovate and to create the new products and processes that give (it) an edge in this very competitive global economy."

He noted that, like hundreds of other companies in Oregon, "ESCO needs people who have both a command of certain specific skills and robust problem-solving and communication skills." And those are precisely the skills and abilities a good liberal education develops in students.

Employers Demand Broad Skill Sets

A recent national employer survey commissioned by AAC&U found that employers believe that colleges—including community colleges—can best prepare graduates for long-term career success by helping them develop both a broad range of skills and knowledge and in-depth skills in a specific field. They are, in fact, now demanding that their employees use a much broader set of skills and have higher levels of learning and knowledge than in the past.

These rising demands are placing increased pressures on all kinds of institutions, but especially on our nation's community colleges. The good news is that institutions like Lane and many others are rising to the challenge and inventing new ways to ensure that, whatever program or educational pathway students choose, they can begin to develop these broad skills and abilities at a community college.

With programs like learning communities, service learning, and cooperative education, community colleges are building ladders of opportunity that will allow students to quickly become prepared for today's workplace while also being positioned for the lifelong learning they will need over the long haul. Continuing to develop and maintain these kinds of innovative educational practices, however, is not easy—especially for the notoriously under-resourced community college sector.

As community colleges struggle in these tight economic times just to keep pace with increasing student demand, we must keep our focused commitment on what a quality education really is in the 21st century. It must include both attention to practical, career and technical programs and a commitment to the broad, contextual knowledge and intellectual skills developed by a liberal education, including such things as the ability to analyze and apply reason to problems as they arise, to accurately interpret new information, and to apply these skills to novel problems.

Community colleges provide a solid grounding in liberal education to all students, including those students pursuing technical degrees.

As we continue to work to serve and graduate more students in these challenging times, community college leaders must also make the case for our continued value to our communities and to the nation's economic and democratic future. As we do so, we must keep front and center both this quality agenda and our commitment to providing every student a blend of practical and liberal learning. Our integrity and the future success of our students and society depend on nothing less.

SIX

High School Career and Technical Education Takes Time Away from Other Studies

Sarah Butrymowicz

In the following viewpoint Sarah Butrymowicz describes the reaction of parents in California's San Diego Unified School District when school officials announced plans to require every high school student to take two to four career and technical education (CTE) courses in order to graduate. Educators quoted in the viewpoint contend that the new requirements would help every student be ready for college and a career and that parents' resistance to the requirements showed a lack of understanding of the value of CTE programs. In fact, they argue, CTE courses prepare students for a variety of difficult and prestigious college programs.

Butrymowicz is a staff writer at Columbia University's Hechinger Institute on Education and the Media.

Career and technical education [CTE] has come a long way since the days when students could be steered from academics into hairstyling, auto repairs or carpentry. But that doesn't mean it's easy to sell the concept of having all students take courses in CTE, as it is known.

Take what happened this March [2012] in La Jolla, Calif. Parents rose in protest after the San Diego Unified School District proposed new high school graduation requirements mandating two years of career and technical education courses—or two to four courses. The district would have been the first in the nation to have such a mandate, experts believe. Parents circulated an online protest petition and school officials spent hours in a meeting to assure hundreds of parents that courses like computerized accounting, child development and website design could be in the best interest of all students.

But afterwards, when parent leaders asked the crowd who favored the requirement, every single parent at the meeting voted against it.

The Haves and Have-Nots

District officials were unprepared for the backlash in the affluent neighborhoods north of Interstate 8, the unofficial boundary between the haves and have-nots of the district. Just two years earlier, the school system passed a mandate—supported by the community—to make all students complete a set of courses required for entry to one of the state's university systems.

They viewed career and technical education courses as a logical extension of their goal to get all students "college and career ready," said Sid Salazar, the district's assistant superintendent for instructional support services. Attending college was once the sole way students could prepare for some professions but opportunities now exist in high school under an expanded definition of career and technical education.

The parents, though, argued that college-bound students wouldn't be helped by taking career and technical education classes. As one parent wrote on an online petition that garnered 1,326 signatures in 21 days: "If you force the children of . . . highly intelligent and very academic parents to take less-rigorous VoTech coursework, you will hurt their chances of admission to undergrad and grad school."

As San Diego demonstrated, despite more than a decade of efforts to revamp its image, technical education still battles a negative reputation. While college-prep graduation requirements are spreading rapidly in California, many affluent parents, and low-income parents who fear their child is being sold short, balk at technical education and assume it won't lead to college.

Benefits for All Students

Advocates are trying to convince people it's not an either-or situation. They argue that although many career and technical fields do not require more than a certificate or an associate's degree, CTE courses can be useful even to those on the four-year university path, including students preparing for professions like teaching and engineering.

Advocates also point to data from the U.S. Department of Education demonstrating that those who concentrate in career and technical education classes in high school are more likely to graduate from high school: 90 percent earned their diploma in the 2007–2008 school year, compared with about 75 percent over all. And nearly 80 percent of those students enroll in post-secondary education within two years of high school graduation.

"There's always been a saying in the field that public attitude toward career and technical education—and I think this is accurate—[is] it's great but for someone else's kids," said Kenneth Gray, an emeritus professor of education at Penn State, who has written extensively about the role of career and technical courses in high school. "I'm convinced that for a whole lot of people, they would much rather have their kid go to Yale and turn out to be a bum than go into career and technical education and be successful."

Gray added, however, that mandating it for all was not a solution. "To say everyone has to take it is as ridiculous in my view as saying everyone has to take calculus," he said.

A Public Relations Problem

Last year [2011], the National Association of State Directors of Career Technical Education Consortium hired an outside communications firm and launched its second major PR [public rela-

Over 92 percent of California's secondary CTE graduates were employed, in the military, or in postsecondary education or advanced training within six months after graduation in 2009–2010.

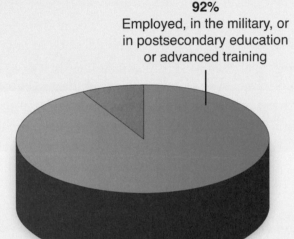

92%
Employed, in the military, or in postsecondary education or advanced training

Taken from: National Association of State Directors of Career Technical Education Consortium. "CTE State Snapshots," 2012. www.careertech.org.

tions] move in as many decades. The new publicity campaign aims to demonstrate CTE's links to college and the workforce. But when Kimberly Green, the consortium's executive director, performs her personal litmus test—chatting with people on airplanes about her job—she still gets a similar response: "I'm so glad people have a place to go that's not . . . college."

"I wouldn't say the tide has turned," she said. "The label is still a barrier."

It's not the only issue. Many San Diego parents worried about the limited amount of time in the school day, a problem even the staunchest technical education proponents recognize.

"It's not that we were against the career technical courses themselves, we were against making them a requirement," said Fran Shrimp, a parent leader in San Diego who organized the petition against mandating the courses. "Getting accepted into a good college is so competitive that students need to pack their schedules with the most challenging courses available just to be in the running."

Vocational education—as it used to be called—was a means of tracking students who were not going to college. A generation ago, that education enabled grads to enter the middle class with just a high school diploma. In the 1970s and '80s, the economy began requiring more skilled workers and middle-class America became more convinced of the importance of college, said Anthony Carnevale, director of the Georgetown University Center on Education and the Workforce. By the mid-1980s, the arguments against tracking flourished and the calls of "college for all" began.

About 10 years ago, responding to the changing economy and attempting to shed its bad reputation, vocational education became career and technical education. But advocates are still trying to cement the name change into the American lexicon. "Career and technical education meant something different than vocational education," Green said. "It's academics plus technical instruction."

Top-Quality Programs

The quality and availability of the programs vary. At the top end, students in medical courses might spend time at a hospital, learning key vocabulary and technical skills like drawing blood. Students can learn engineering design programs on computers or spend time taking apart electronics to learn how they work. Students in cosmetology programs might study the chemistry behind hair dye.

Information technology, marketing and business management all fall under technical education's new wide umbrella, as do professions like engineering and architecture. Even the old standards, like auto shop, require a level of academics not needed in the past to keep up with increasingly computerized car engines, Green said.

At Patrick Henry High School in San Diego, if students pass all three pre-engineering courses offered, they'll be automatically admitted into San Diego State's engineering program. At the high school's teaching academy, students work with nursery school children and graduate with just two community college credits shy of earning a preschool teacher's license.

San Diego district officials held up programs like these as examples and argued that more than 90 percent of students were already taking at least one of the 158 technical education courses the district offered. And 60 of them were approved by the state university systems to count toward college admission.

The parents were not swayed, concerned about having time in their children's schedules for electives and Advanced Placement courses. "If the program is successful on its own, why change it?" Shrimp said. She also noted that the same set of CTE courses are not offered at each high school, meaning students might be relegated to classes that don't interest them.

Within a month of meeting with parents in La Jolla, the San Diego Board of Education voted to rescind the requirements.

A Major Setback

Scott Himelstein, director of the University of San Diego's Center for Education Policy and Law and former deputy secretary of Education for California, viewed the vote as a "major setback." Policymakers need to gather the political courage to start promoting career and technical education, given that only a quarter of high schoolers in the state will go on to get a four-year degree, he said. Nationally, more than 30 percent of adults have at least a bachelor's degree, according to census figures.

One compromise, according to Himelstein, is to approve more career and technical courses to count towards the University of California and California State University systems' so-called "a–g" entry requirements. This list of courses, which San Diego

Career and technical education courses prepare students for a variety of college programs.

and several other districts have adopted as graduation requirements, spell out what courses students must complete in high school to be eligible for admittance to the universities, including core subjects like math and English, as well as a certain number of electives.

The university systems approve courses on an individual basis, meaning each district's biology or calculus course must get a separate approval. Ten years ago, no career and technical classes were approved for a–g, according to Gary Hoachlander, president of ConnectEd, a California group that works with nine districts to create career-oriented high school and college trajectories for students. Now, there are some 10,000 a–g courses across all the state's districts.

The vast majority count as electives. Often career and technical science classes, such as environmental science or agricultural science, won't count as an a–g science credit. "That's where I think there's still a lot of work to do," Hoachlander said.

SEVEN

High School Programs Must Do a Better Job of Preparing Students for College

Arne Duncan

> In the following viewpoint US secretary of education Arne Duncan argues that career and technical education (CTE) must gain more respect and more funding, but that both must be contingent on the programs changing to reflect the demands of the twenty-first century. Specifically, Duncan states, high school CTE programs must go beyond preparing students for particular jobs and give them the academic skills they will need to succeed in college right away—without the need for remedial courses. When CTE programs can demonstrate that they are preparing students for college and careers, he concludes, the federal government will be ready to give them more financial support.

We're at a time when Americans everywhere are asking some very tough questions about education. But it all comes down to one: What will it take to dramatically improve public education in America?

To this end, there's an urgent need to re-imagine and remake career and technical education. CTE has an enormous, if often

Arne Duncan, "Rigor, Relevance, and the Future of CTE: Remarks of U.S. Secretary of Education Arne Duncan," United States Department of Education, April 19, 2011.

overlooked impact on students, school systems, and our ability to prosper as a nation.

At the same time, we need a frank discussion about the shortcomings of the current system. At the heart of the matter is that CTE programs need to strengthen their rigor and relevance—and deliver better outcomes for students.

Today I want to help define the conversation about the future of CTE.

For far too long, CTE has been a neglected part of the reform movement. That neglect has to stop.

But focusing more attention on CTE also means committing to increased innovation, rigor and results. At a time when local, state, and federal governments are facing tremendous budget pressure, CTE advocates must make a compelling case for continued funding.

To accomplish these things, the mission of CTE will have to change. It can no longer simply be about earning a diploma and landing a job after high school. The goal of CTE 2.0 should be that students earn a postsecondary credential or an industry-recognized certification—and land a job that leads to a successful career.

A New Standard: Career-Readiness

There is a lot of talk these days about the need to boost college and career-readiness. But the truth is that most people,—and I include myself here—have focused primarily on college-readiness. Too often, career-readiness is an afterthought.

One reason for this is that it seems easier to define college-readiness than career-readiness, even if there is a great deal of overlap.

At the [U.S.] Department [of Education], we define a college-ready student as someone who has the knowledge and skills to succeed in credit-bearing courses from day one, without remediation. That standard must be the new bar for success for all high schools, and for all students—instead of the old goal of getting students a diploma.

The bar for a career-ready student is just as demanding. CTE students also must have the academic skills to be able to engage in postsecondary education and training without the need for remediation. The cause of strengthening CTE programs should never be an excuse for reducing rigor and tracking students away from pursuing a college degree.

Students pursuing non-degree postsecondary credentials still need college-ready academic skills. Airplane mechanics and X-ray technicians may not need a four-year degree. But they do need advanced math skills, including Algebra 2.

Yet a career-ready student must also have the knowledge and skills that employers need from day one. That means having critical thinking and problem-solving skills, an ability to synthesize information, solid communication skills, and the ability to work well on a team.

Public Schools Must Prepare Students

So I start with the basic premise that it is the responsibility of K–12 [kindergarten through grade twelve] educators to prepare all students for both college and a career. This must be "both/and", not "either/or." High school graduates—not the educational system—should be choosing the postsecondary and career paths they want to pursue.

For too long, public schools have gotten this wrong. Too often, the K–12 system made these choices for children, tracking them into dead-end courses—instead of providing them with the skills necessary to succeed in college and careers and the guidance students needed to make good decisions about their future.

Students need the same set of skills for both college and the workplace, particularly in reading and math. And it's the job of the K–12 system to prepare them for both options. In our globally-competitive, knowledge-based economy, all Americans are likely to face the challenge of a lifetime of continued learning. And all need a common core of skills.

Today, these career skills are poorly-defined in America's K–12 system. But they are one of the universal hallmarks of world-class education systems in the 21st century.

Education secretary Arne Duncan says that when CTE programs can demonstrate that they are preparing students for college and careers the federal government will be ready to distribute more funds to them.

U.S. students will need both the hard skills of math and English language arts and science, and the soft career skills, to thrive in our flattened world. In fact, many of the nations that are outperforming us educationally today have far more effective career and technical education systems than the United States.

Advice from the President

To be a winner in the future, President [Barack] Obama has urged every American to get at least a year of higher education or post-secondary career training. "Whatever the training may be," the President says, "every American will need to get more than a high school diploma."

In effect, the President has suggested that every American earn a minimum of two pieces of paper—a high school diploma, and a degree or industry-recognized certification. In the years ahead, young adults are likely to need those two credentials to secure a good job. That will become the ticket to success and a positive future.

For all its importance, the role that CTE plays in building the nation's economic vitality often gets overlooked. Too many educators assume that career and technical training is for the last century, not this one. Many reformers treat CTE as old school—rather than as a potential source of cutting-edge preparation for careers.

In the new CTE we are working toward, all career and technical programs would serve as viable and rigorous pathways to postsecondary and workforce success. . . .

I want to acknowledge that this—like all education reform—is extremely hard work. But it is absolutely essential that the CTE community take on this challenge.

Funding Follows Success

I don't need to remind you that these are extraordinarily difficult fiscal times at the local, state, and federal levels.

With few exceptions, states have yet to recover from the Great Recession. Many communities are still feeling the pain of the housing market crash in the form of lost property tax revenue. And at the federal level, the President and Congress are engaged in a serious effort to reduce the federal deficit.

In this environment, programs that promise to deliver results will continue to thrive. But others will have a difficult time maintaining their funding.

Right now, CTE programs receiving federal support under the [Carl D.] Perkins [Career and Technical Education] Act [of 2006] need to make a convincing case for funding. That starts by showing that you're improving student outcomes. And there's no better data to demonstrate that than by identifying how many students are going on to postsecondary education and starting careers in the pathway they studied.

We should be able to look at every CTE program in your state and answer how many students graduate from high school and transition successfully into and complete at least one year of postsecondary education or training. If a program cannot deliver these outcomes or provide these data, then we should re-tool it. . . .

Once CTE programs deliver on the promise of truly preparing students for success in college and careers, their successes will make a compelling case for further investment. I will be your strongest advocate for ensuring that these programs receive the funding they need to help students achieve.

I am confident that the CTE community can make that happen. I believe we can take CTE reforms to scale because we are seeing how these programs can transform the lives of teenagers and adults.

Seeds of Success

I can see the seeds of success across the country.

Northern Virginia Community College has started an early college CTE academy that allows students to graduate with associate degrees in year 13 of school, in high-demand fields like science, technology, engineering and math, or STEM. And, they are working with schools to help students explore STEM careers, in as early as eighth grade.

In Washington State, the Granite Falls High School Shop Girls built homemade cars focused on fuel-efficient designs. They designed a diesel-powered vehicle that got a staggering 470 miles to the gallon. They called their car the "Iron Maiden." You won't

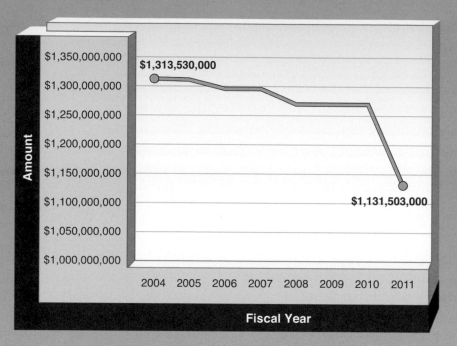

Declining Federal Support

Since 2004 federal appropriations for career and technical education have decreased.

$1,313,530,000

$1,131,503,000

Amount

Fiscal Year

2004 2005 2006 2007 2008 2009 2010 2011

Taken from: National Association of State Directors of Career Technical Education, 2012. www.careertech.org.

be surprised to hear that the Iron Maiden won the diesel fuel design competition—and the cash award that went with it.

And last month [March 2011], the President and I visited TechBoston Academy—a school where students are studying a rigorous curriculum that includes four years each of math, science, and technology. These courses combine the academic rigor of a college-prep curriculum with real-life experiences in Web development, entrepreneurship, and criminal forensics.

Students can take Advanced Placement courses as well as classes that prepare them to complete professional certificates recognized by industry leaders such as Microsoft and Cisco Networking.

Northern Virginia Community College, Granite Falls High School, and TechBoston—these are examples of excellence that I want to become the norm. They provide rigor and relevance. They offer a springboard to higher education and postsecondary training—not a dead-end.

Let's all work together to make this happen.

Thank you.

EIGHT

Low-Income and Minority Students Are Being Squeezed Out of Higher Education

Gary Rhoades

In the following viewpoint Gary Rhoades explains how the shrinking economy and the declining amount of financial support for community colleges disproportionately hurts low-income and minority students. With tuition costs rising at all types of colleges, even upper-income students, Rhoades points out, are increasingly choosing to begin their college careers at less-expensive community colleges, making the competition for community college seats stiffer. And low-income students, he concludes, are more likely to give up on college entirely if the costs go too high.

Rhoades is a professor and the director of the Center for the Study of Higher Education at the University of Arizona.

Some press coverage about community colleges focuses on how they are getting squeezed by budget cuts amidst enrollment pressure. The sense is that reduced enrollments will give colleges breathing room after years of rapid growth. But who is getting squeezed out? That question cuts to the core of these open access colleges.

The community college is a quintessentially American creation. It affords opportunity to those (including very academically-able students) who cannot afford other types of colleges, to those who are not qualified for more selective institutions, and to those who want a second chance at college. Within each of these segments of potential students, there is burgeoning demand; growing student markets are not being served.

Community colleges are "Democracy's open door," postsecondary education's Statue of Liberty, an entrée to pursuing the American dream regardless of one's life circumstances. They are an expression of America's promise that money and background will not *determine* one's life chances (though they do affect those chances). All the more important, then, to consider patterns in who is being denied access to community colleges, in whose dreams are being deferred.

One way to consider whether there are patterns in whose college opportunities are being closed out is to ask whether disproportionate numbers of students in a particular ethnic, class, or age category are being denied access. Answering this question requires more than monitoring changes in numbers of lower-income students and students of color from one year to the next, for such changes might be caused by demographic changes, or by changes in applicant pools, independently of who is being turned away.

Rationing Access to Higher Education

Different metaphors may be used to describe rationing access to colleges. Some seem more innocuous than others:

> The big story is the number of first-time students—the recent high school graduates—who are being squeezed out, says Paul Steenhausen, community college expert for the Legislative Analyst's Office. "I liken it to an unfortunate game of musical chairs where there's not enough chairs for participants and when the music stops, it's the new guy every time who winds up without a seat."

The above analogy frames the situation as one of random chance, of new, young applicants losing out, without reference to the economic or ethnic background of these youth. Policy makers are increasingly adopting this framing.

Other metaphors point to a pattern that is deeply problematic in a democracy. The headline, "Class rationing coming to California?" conveys a double entendre and harsh reality about what is happening in community colleges—we are rationing classes; and we are sorting students by social class. The article notes: "California community colleges are supposed to be an affordable way for state residents to get a higher education. . . . [They] have long been touted as a way to break the poverty cycle, allowing first-generation college students to find good jobs and income once their college education is completed." Given the history of community colleges, and the future growth demographic in students, rationing that reduces lower-income students' access is a substantial, problematic shift. . . .

The Cascade Effect and Community Colleges

The National Student Clearinghouse's (NSC) August 2011 report on enrollments points to a "cascade effect" that is affecting who is enrolling in community colleges:

> The shift in traditional age student enrollments toward the public two-year sector during the recession suggests, furthermore, that some students may have enrolled in community colleges as a means of saving money. In addition to seeing general increases in their enrollments, community colleges saw increases in their full-time enrollments—suggesting the possibility that students who might otherwise have attended four-year institutions full-time were instead enrolling in greater numbers at community colleges.

> Larger proportions of full-time students and of students in four-year colleges are middle- and upper-middle class, whereas larger proportions of students in community colleges are part-time and

High-Income Students Choose Community Colleges

In 2010–2011 more students from families earning one hundred thousand dollars or more attended community colleges than the year before, according to an annual survey by the student loan corporation Sallie Mae.

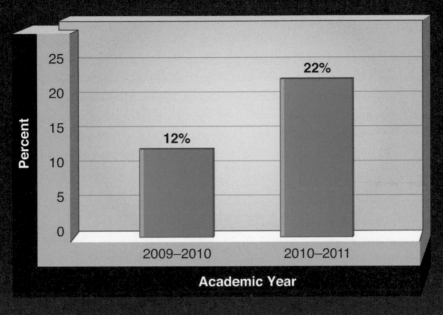

Taken from: Sallie Mae. "How America Pays for College 2011," August 2011. https://www1.salliemae.com.

working class. There may be a social class dimension to the cascade effect stemming from large tuition increases in four-year institutions. Unfortunately, the NSC does not gather data on students' household income or on their race/ethnicity.

As tuition continues to escalate, particularly in public universities, the pressure on community colleges increases. Tuition spikes in public four-year institutions are associated with enrollment declines in subsequent years. Thus, it is likely that students who formerly would have enrolled in a four-year institution are now competing with students for whom community college is really the only choice. . . .

Rising Tuition in Community Colleges

Another dimension of the cresting wave phenomenon is that students are getting squeezed by higher tuition as colleges are getting squeezed by cuts in public funding. A survey of state community college directors yielded a median prediction of 5.6% tuition increases at community colleges for FY [fiscal year] 2012: the previous year, 86% of the respondents reported tuition increases, yielding a national average of 5.8%. That is on top of a 3.6% tuition increase ($113) in 2008–2009. That same year, state and local appropriations to community colleges fell, on average, $448 per student. The tuition increases are not keeping pace with decreased public funding.

Such tuition increases may seem relatively small but the increases are more than double the inflation rate of the Higher Education Price Index and other measures of inflation. The significance of such increases, and of Pell Grants to counter them, is highlighted by a recent national report. . . .

The price sensitivity of many community college students has an impact on levels of student debt in this sector. Speculation that a low level of student debt in community colleges means cost is not a problem misses the point. Relatively low percentages of community college students in debt (13%) reflects not just lower tuition costs, but also the fact that rather than going into debt to pay higher tuition, many students simply do not attend, or drop out. They do not so much go into debt as they just don't go.

Who Gets Squeezed Out?

Up to this point, this [viewpoint] has explored possible disparate impacts on who gets turned away from or is not applying to community colleges. But there is another way to gauge who is getting squeezed out when doors are closed. Consider the patterns in who goes to community colleges, and from that infer the collective effects on access of closing the open door.

The opening line of a recent study of low-income students' access to higher education puts the matter starkly: "College choice in the United States is stratified by family income. Students with the lowest family incomes are relatively concentrated in private, for-profit institutions and public two-year colleges." In 2003–2004, at community colleges, 16% of the dependent students had household incomes less than $20,000 compared to 10% each in public and private universities. Focusing on income quartiles, the numbers are even more disparate. . . .

Racial stratification of enrollments in higher education exists not only among different types of colleges, but also among community colleges. Recent reports by the UCLA [University of California, Los Angeles] Civil Rights Project reveals that although "nearly three-quarters of Latinos and two-thirds of African-American high school students who pursue higher education in California start at

The rising cost of postsecondary education has forced students to begin their college careers at less-expensive community colleges. Low-income students are more likely to give up college entirely because of the cost.

a community college; in 2010 only 20% of students transferring to four-year institutions were Latino or Black." Community colleges that transferred the largest proportions of students had the lowest concentration of students from underrepresented populations, whereas those with the highest concentrations had the lowest transfer rates.

In the words of Patrick M. Callan, President of the National Center for Public Policy and Higher Education, "Higher education is more stratified than it's ever been." Our current policy path, of continued cuts in state support and continued increases in tuition, will only increase that stratification in the future. That is particularly true when one considers the growth demographic in elementary and secondary schools of lower-income students and students of color.

NINE

Expecting "College for All" Is Misguided

James R. Stone

In the following viewpoint James R. Stone counters President Barack Obama's 2012 call for "college for all." Stone points out that many low-wage jobs still do not require higher education and that changes in manufacturing will keep wages for many workers low regardless of their college degrees. The American education system, he argues, must make high school more meaningful for the many students who will never attend college and must develop quicker paths for students who want to begin training for careers. Career and technical education (CTE) programs, he concludes, should keep students engaged by offering work-based learning as early as middle school.

Stone is a professor and the director of the National Research Center for Career and Technical Education at the University of Louisville in Kentucky.

The current debate about "college for all" centers on a [February 25, 2012,] speech made by President [Barack] Obama in Troy, MI, in which he argued that all young people should get at least some post-high school education or training. Republican presidential primary candidate Rick Santorum, in a misreading of Obama's remarks, responded with a focus on four-year degrees alone—suggesting, among other things, that four-year college degrees are overrated and that the president's emphasis on college devalued working people without such degrees. The political chatter around this particular back-and-forth continues, but the issue of "college for all" has rightly raised some serious issues about the content and direction of U.S. education policy both at the high school and post-secondary levels.

Statistics seem to show that the college-educated graduates of four-year institutions earn more money and experience less unemployment than their non-college-educated peers. This has fueled the argument that college is the surest path—perhaps the only path—into the middle class. But the argument confuses correlation with causality. What if every U.S. citizen obtained a community college or university degree? Would that really do anything to alter wage rates at Starbucks, or increase salaries for home healthcare aides (an occupation projected to enjoy the highest demand over the next decade)? Of course not.

Among other factors, wages have been profoundly affected by a labor market transformed through digital technology. [Erik] Brynjolfsson and [Andrew] McAfee's *Race Against the Machine* argued that digital technology is increasingly displacing humans in the completion of sophisticated tasks. Although this phenomenon is not new, it is different than in the past. Where once it took 125 [Ford] assembly workers to produce a Model T [manufactured between 1908 and 1927], it takes only 13 to produce the Ford Escape—this is old news. What's new is RFID [radio-frequency identification] scanners and robots replacing grocery store clerks; armies of lawyers being replaced by software; a computer beating a human on the popular *Jeopardy* show.

Unions are another mediating factor; they have suffered tremendous losses over the past decades and private sector density is below 7 percent. This has had a major impact on working-class wages. As reported in a recent *Forbes* article, German auto workers earn an average of $67.14 per hour, whereas their U.S. counterparts average only $33.77. In non-union auto plants in

Conservative presidential hopeful Rick Santorum (pictured) took issue with President Barack Obama's remarks about "college for all," saying that four-year college degrees are overrated and that Obama showed disrespect for working people who do not have such degrees.

Tennessee, workers start at $14.50. Non-union housekeepers earn $8 an hour, unionized housekeepers $22 an hour. In this context, the lack of a college degree is not a sufficient explanation for the difference between a middle-class income and a near-poverty income. Skills differences are not the full explanation for wage differences. Although education and skills play a role, technology and labor market structures explain much more.

Three Major Challenges

But let's assume that all youth should get some college education. The less than 75 percent of youth who successfully complete high school face three major challenges: First, higher education costs are increasing. Forty-one states are reported to be cutting higher education support. Florida, as recently reported in the *New York Times*, is planning to cut higher education funding by a draconian $250 million and to allow universities to raise tuition by 8 to 15 percent, putting higher education out of reach for many.

Second, the capacity of postsecondary education and training programs in high-demand fields, such as healthcare, is restricted by the limited number of internship and apprenticeship placements available to such programs. There is also a disconnect between popular programs and labor market opportunity. In the early 2000s, for example, demand for forensic science programs—spurred by the popularity of shows such as *CSI*—far outstripped program capacity and labor market demand. Community colleges too often respond to this rising student demand by expanding their programs, without respect to real labor market opportunities.

Third and finally, there is the challenge of student capability—that is, students' ability to learn in a traditional college setting. Many students who do finish high school graduate without the academic skills needed to pass college placement tests. Such students are shunted into remedial courses, where many find themselves on a pathway to nowhere. Some community colleges have responded by trying to move lower-skilled students directly into occupational programs, but this remains a challenge, especially in an era of reduced resources.

Why Must Students Wait?

So what should we do for the many young people who will never go to college? Why must they wait until after high school graduation—when individual and societal costs increase so dramatically—in order to prepare for a productive adulthood?

We must make high school matter for these youth.

Doing so requires rethinking how we organize learning opportunities to provide rigorous, world-class technical education to the many disengaged youth now suffering through ever-increasing academic requirements. The National Center on Education and the Economy's *Tough Choices, Tough Times* argued for a 10th-grade board examination that would allow successful students to move directly into community college-level technical programs or to continue in a true college preparatory program to a second level of examinations. Implementing this intriguing model would require major systemic changes in public education.

For example, in Georgetown, KY, Toyota has worked with local education systems to create a compelling, rigorous and relevant manufacturing career pathway—one that takes students from high school to the local community college to four-year college programs in engineering or manufacturing management and the promise of employment with Toyota. This innovative program of intensive work-based learning (WBL) and rigorous academics is based in one of the most sophisticated manufacturing operations in the world.

In addition to models such as these, we can make high school matter by retooling existing Career and Technical Education (CTE) programs to reflect both anticipated labor market opportunities and the education that leads to them. Essential components of a retooled CTE system include intensive career development opportunities that begin no later than middle school; internships, apprenticeships, and other WBL that engage youth with the labor market; and curricula that integrate academic knowledge with technical skills, yielding recognized industry credentials.

TEN

Obtaining a Four-Year Degree Is Not Worth the Cost

Sarah Kaufman

In the following viewpoint by Sarah Kaufman a hedge fund manager and father argues that college is not the best or the only way to develop the skills needed for a successful career. Money intended for college tuition, he says, would yield a higher return if it were simply invested. An economist interviewed in the viewpoint points out that while some college majors lead to jobs that pay well, many do not, and many recent college graduates are having trouble finding jobs. Young people, the viewpoint concludes, might be better off following the examples of the successful entrepreneurs who left college and started their own businesses.

Kaufman is a Pulitzer Prize–winning writer for the *Washington Post.*

Across the region and around the country, parents are kissing their college-bound kids—and potentially up to $200,000 in tuition, room and board—goodbye.

Especially in the supremely well-educated Washington [D.C.] area, this is expected. It's a rite of passage, part of an orderly progression toward success.

Or is it . . . *herd mentality?*

Hear this, high achievers: If you crunch the numbers, some experts say, college is a bad investment.

"You've been fooled into thinking there's no other way for my kid to get a job . . . or learn critical thinking or make social connections," hedge fund manager James Altucher says.

Altucher, president of Formula Capital, says he sees people making bad investment decisions all the time—and one of them is paying for college.

College Is Overrated

College is overrated, he says: In most cases, what you get out of it is not worth the money, and there are cheaper and better ways to get an education. Altucher says he's not planning to send his two daughters to college.

"My plan is to encourage them to pursue a dream, at least initially," Altucher, 42, says. "Travel or do something creative or start a business. . . . Whether they succeed or fail, it'll be an interesting life experience. They'll meet people, they'll learn the value of money."

Certainly, you'd be forgiven for thinking this argument reeks of elitism. After all, Altucher is an Ivy Leaguer. He's rolling in dough. Easy for *him* to pooh-pooh the status quo.

But, it turns out, his anti-college ideas stem from personal experience. After his first year at Cornell University, Altucher says his parents lost money and couldn't afford tuition. So he paid his own way, working 60 hours a week delivering pizza and tutoring, on top of his course load.

He left Cornell thousands of dollars in debt. He also left with a degree in computer science. But it took failing at several investment schemes, losing large sums of money and then studying the stock market on his own—analyzing [billionaire business tycoon] Warren Buffett's decisions so closely he ended up writing a book

The hefty price tag of a college degree has some experts worried that its benefits are fading.

about him—for Altucher to learn enough about the financial world to survive in it. He thinks he would have been better off getting the real-world lessons earlier, rather than thrashing himself to pay for school and shouldering so much debt.

Better Ways to Use Money

It's cold comfort, but the loans put him in good company: Hundreds of billions of dollars of national student-loan debt has now overtaken American credit-card debt, the *Wall Street Journal* recently reported, using numbers compiled by FinAid.org, a Web site for college financial aid information.

"There's a billion other things you could do with your money," Altucher says. One option: Invest the money you'd spend on tuition in Treasury bills for your child's retirement. According to Altucher, $200,000 earning 5 percent a year over 50 years would amount to $2.8 million.

Few families have that kind of money lying around. But if you can give your child $10,000 or so to start his own business, Altucher says, your child will reap practical lessons never taught in a classroom. Later, when he's more mature and focused, college might be more meaningful.

The hefty price tag of a college degree has some experts worried that its benefits are fading.

"I think it makes less sense for more families than it did five years ago," says Richard Vedder, an economics professor at Ohio University who has been studying education issues. "It's become more and more problematic about whether people should be going to college."

That applies not just to astronomically priced private schools but to state schools as well, where tuitions have spiked. Student loans can postpone the pain of paying, but they come due when many young adults are at their most financially vulnerable, and default rates are high. Even community colleges, while helping some to keep costs down, prompt many to take out loans—which can land them in severe credit trouble.

Struggling to Pay Back Loans

According to a report in the *Chronicle of Higher Education*, 31 percent of loans made to community college students are in default. (The same report found that 25 percent of all government student loans default.) Default on a student loan and face dire consequences, beyond a bad credit record—which can tarnish hopes of getting a car, an apartment or even a job: Uncle Sam can claim your tax refunds and wages.

Now, take a key argument in favor of getting a four-year degree, the one that says on average, those with one earn more than those without it. Education Department numbers support this: In

2008, the median annual earnings of young adults with bachelor's degrees was $46,000; it was $30,000 for those with high school diplomas or equivalencies. This means that, for those with a bachelor's degree, the middle range of earnings was about 53 percent more than for those holding only a high school diploma.

But a lot of college graduates fall outside the middle range—and many stand to make considerably less.

"If you major in accounting or engineering, you're pretty likely to get a return on your investment," Vedder says. "If you're majoring in anthropology or social work or education, the rate on return is going to be a good deal lower, on average.

"I've talked to some of my own students who've graduated and who are working in grocery stores or Wal-Mart," he says. "The fellow who cut my tree down had a master's degree and was an honors grad."

The unemployment rate among those with bachelor's degrees is at an all-time high. In 1970, when the overall unemployment rate was 4.9 percent, unemployment among college graduates was negligible, at 1.2 percent, Vedder says, citing figures from the Bureau of Labor Statistics. But this year [2010], with the national rate of unemployment at 9.6 percent, unemployment for college graduates has risen to 4.9 percent—more than half the rate of the general population. The bonus for those with degrees is "less pronounced than it used to be," Vedder says.

"The return on investment is clearly lower today than it was five years ago," he says. "The gains for going to college have leveled off."

Before hackles are raised about boiling the salutary effects of higher education down to its cost, there are obvious disclaimers: Education is a priceless thing. Many high-school graduates are not ready for independence and adult responsibilities, and college provides a safe place for them to grow up—for a fee.

Dropout Success Stories

But what about the lessons offered by the success stories that have unspooled along a different path? Dropouts are the toast

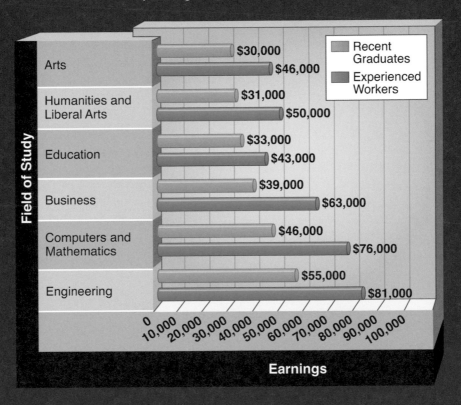

College Majors Not Created Equal

Experienced workers with four-year degrees stand to earn widely different amounts depending on their field of study,

Field of Study

Field of Study	Recent Graduates	Experienced Workers
Arts	$30,000	$46,000
Humanities and Liberal Arts	$31,000	$50,000
Education	$33,000	$43,000
Business	$39,000	$63,000
Computers and Mathematics	$46,000	$76,000
Engineering	$55,000	$81,000

Earnings: 0, 10,000, 20,000, 30,000, 40,000, 50,000, 60,000, 70,000, 80,000, 90,000, 100,000

Taken from: Anthony Carnevale, Bam Cheah, and Jeff Strohl. "Hard Times: College Majors, Unemployment and Earnings." Georgetown University Center on Education and the Workforce, 2012. www9.georgetown.edu.

of the dot-com world. To the non-degreed billionaires' club headed by Microsoft's Bill Gates (Harvard's most famous quitter) and Apple's Steve Jobs (left Oregon's Reed College after a single semester), add: Michael Dell (founder of Dell Computers, University of Texas dropout), Microsoft co-founder and Seattle Seahawks owner Paul Allen (quit Washington State University) and Larry Ellison (founder of Oracle Systems, gave up on the University of Illinois).

Success sans sheepskin isn't only for the technology set.

David Geffen, co-founder of DreamWorks, bowed out of several schools, including the University of Texas.

Redskins owner Daniel Snyder dropped out of the University of Maryland.

Barry Gossett, chief executive of Baltimore's Acton Mobile Industries, builders of temporary trailers, also left Maryland without a degree. (No hard feelings, apparently: In 2007, he donated $10 million to the school.)

Perhaps these are unique individuals in whom a driving entrepreneurial spirit outstripped the plodding pace of book learning.

Or perhaps they point to a new model.

ELEVEN

Career and Technical Programs Can Get Dropouts Back on Track

Dorothy Stoneman

In the following viewpoint, originally given as testimony before a US House of Representatives committee, Dorothy Stoneman describes a federal program called YouthBuild, sponsored by the US Department of Labor, and the program's success at providing job skills in construction and a basic education to young people who did not complete high school. Stoneman argues that YouthBuild succeeds in bringing disadvantaged young people into responsible careers and lives because it addresses the students' personal, social, and educational needs together. She concludes that YouthBuild is less expensive than sending a troubled young person to prison or to college and that Congress should appropriate more money to continue and expand the program.

Stoneman is chairman of the National YouthBuild Coalition.

Since 1992, when the first federal YouthBuild authorization was passed, 84,000 YouthBuild students have produced 18,000 units of affordable housing in over 225 of America's poorest urban

Dorothy Stoneman, "The YouthBuild Program as an Example of What Works for Out-of-School Unemployed Low Income Youth," U.S. House of Representatives Education and Labor Committee Hearing on Ensuring Economic Opportunity for Young Americans, October 1, 2009, pp. 1–4, 6.

and rural communities, while pursuing a high school diploma or GED [general equivalency diploma] and preparing for college or for careers in construction, and internalizing the values and skills to serve as good citizens.

DOL's [the US Department of Labor's] YouthBuild program is the only federal program that provides disconnected young adults an immediately productive role in the community while also providing equal measures of basic education toward a diploma or GED, skills training toward a decent paying job, leadership development toward civic engagement, adult mentorship toward overcoming personal problems, and participation in a supportive mini-community with a positive set of values. It attracts the most disadvantaged youth, and produces a reliable shift in their values, attitudes, skills and personal identity. . . .

Radically Changing Lives

YouthBuild programs welcome the most disadvantaged youth: 93% without a diploma; 40% adjudicated; 73% young men; 78% Black, Latino, or Native American. All are poor; many have been gang affiliated; most have almost no healthy family support. Yet just about half of those who enroll in YouthBuild radically change their lives.

A Brandeis University study of 800 YouthBuild graduates up to seven years after graduation found that 75% were either in college or employed at jobs averaging $10/hour. 65% said they expected to live longer as a result of YouthBuild—an average of 32 years longer. In fact, most disconnected young men do not expect to live beyond age 25. Graduates often say, "Without YouthBuild I would probably be dead or in jail. Instead I am working, going to college, taking care of my children, aiming to own my own home. I love YouthBuild. It changed my life."

How and Why YouthBuild Works

In YouthBuild programs low-income 16 to 24 year olds enroll full-time for about a year. They split their time evenly between the

The percentage of young people aged sixteen to twenty-four who are not in high school and who have not earned a diploma or an equivalency certificate has declined over the past four decades, according to Child Trends Data Bank.

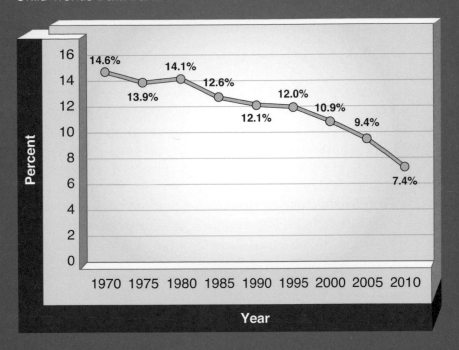

Taken from: "High School Dropout Rates: Indicators on Children and Youth." Child Trends Data bank, April 2012. www.childtrendsdatabank.org.

YouthBuild alternative school where they work toward their GED or diploma in a highly individualized and supportive classroom, and the construction site where they build affordable housing for homeless and low-income people under skilled supervisors, often union journeymen, who teach them the skills they need to succeed at work. They generally alternate a week in the classroom with a week on the construction site. They are paid minimum wage for their work building homes. Increasingly these homes are built green and the students are obtaining industry-recognized certifications and learning the skills to be employed in the new green economy.

At the same time, students are offered personal counseling to help solve all manner of personal problems. They are members of a supportive community of peers and adults dedicated to each other's success. They internalize the ethic of service and are given leadership roles. They recite a daily pledge to become responsible caring leaders who respect others as they would like to be respected. For most, it is the first time they have experienced a safe, healthy, supportive, goal-oriented community that respects their inherent value and draws out their talents. There are many very talented young people who have lost their way, and who can become a real resource to their communities if offered the right opportunities to take charge of their lives.

YouthBuild students work on assembling housing components. YouthBuild helps low-income youths work toward a GED or high school diploma while being trained in construction skills.

YouthBuild creates small manageable communities of 30 to 200 students, with a high staff to student ratio. If you ask the students why YouthBuild worked for them, they always say, "It's the staff and the teachers. They care about us. They teach us how to act. They give us structure and help us set our own goals, and they show us that they really care that we succeed. Nobody ever cared about me like this before. I came to YouthBuild looking for a job and a GED, but I found a family and a future."

We encourage the staff to show they care by doing things that will surprise the students. For example, when a student doesn't show up, someone will call him, or go knock on his door. When a student is found through random drug testing to be using drugs he will be taken off the construction site and required to get counseling. When a student has to go to court for an offense committed prior to enrollment, a staff member will go with him, and maybe take a group of students dressed in suits to demonstrate social attachment to a respectable group. When he is applying for college, someone will drive him there and if necessary pay the application fee. When he is going for a job interview, someone will make sure he has the proper attire.

A Desire to Give Back

As a result, YouthBuild students develop a deep desire to give back. They want to help others as they have been helped. They become a positive force. As YouthBuild graduate Antoine Bennett once said, "I used to be a menace to my community; now I am a minister to it." Sure enough, Antoine is now the executive director of a local job training program in Sandtown, Baltimore; ten years ago he was in prison for a violent crime.

The act of building homes for people who need them, being seen in the community as a hero instead of a hoodlum, changes their identity and relationship to society. They love making a difference. They love being the ones who are doing something good instead of something bad. They are on the streets with tool belts instead of drugs. For the first time in their lives their grandparents are proud of them and their neighbors admire them. Other young people ask, "How can I do what you are doing? How can I get into YouthBuild?" It's contagious. The result is that in every community 2 to 10 times as many young people apply as can be accepted, purely through word of mouth. In North Philadelphia 1,000 young people apply annually for just 200 openings. Where will the other 800 go? There are precious few options. I have watched them leave the waiting room, crying. . . .

YouthBuild USA's goal is to open the doors of YouthBuild to every youth that is knocking and provide the resources to every community-based agency competent to sponsor a YouthBuild program. Over 1,800 communities have applied for YouthBuild funds and thousands of young people are turned away each year. The [Barack] Obama Administration and our champions in Congress have proposed a steady expansion of YouthBuild to 50,000 young adults per year. I ask your help in making that possible through a steady increase in the YouthBuild appropriation. DOL's YouthBuild program received $120M in FY [fiscal year] '09; to reach 50,000 youth/year it will need $1B[illion]. It does cost about $20,000 per full year per student, but this includes wages for the housing they produce, and is still less than the other full-time options for out-of-school youth: less than the military, college, Job Corps, or prison. The return on investment is enormous. One recent study by Professor Mark Cohen documented that every dollar spent on a court-involved youth in YouthBuild provided a return on investment of at least $10.90. This is an investment worth making.

TWELVE

For-Profit Colleges Are Expensive but Effective

Kevin Carey

In the following viewpoint Kevin Carey describes the increase in the number of for-profit colleges since the 1990s and explains that much of the industry's profit comes from federal grants and loans awarded to students and paid to the colleges as tuition. No one should be surprised or angry over the fact that for-profit colleges make substantial profits, he points out, because the colleges have been successful at attracting low- and middle-income students who can draw on federal funding. This, he concludes, is more good than bad, because the for-profit colleges have found ways to serve students that the private and public nonprofit colleges cannot or will not serve.

Carey is policy director of Education Sector, an independent think tank in Washington, D.C.

Michael Clifford believes that education is the only path to world peace. He never went to college, but sometimes he calls himself "Doctor." [Televangelist] Jerry Falwell is one of his heroes. Clifford has made millions of dollars from government programs but doesn't seem to see the windfall that way. Improbably,

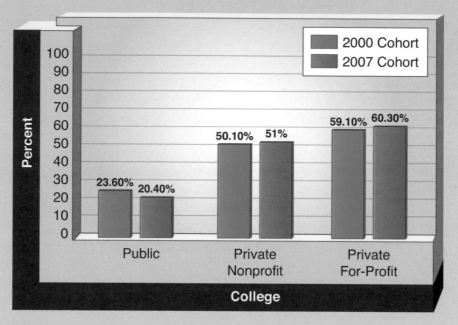

College Graduation Rates: Two-Year Programs

First-time, full-time students who earn an associate's degree or certificate within three years.

Based on data from *The Condition of Education 2012*, US Department of Education.

Taken from: Jordan Weissman. "The One Thing For-Profit Colleges Do Right." *The Atlantic*, June 4, 2012. www.theatlantic.com.

he has come to symbolize the contradictions at the heart of the growing national debate over for-profit higher education.

Until recently, for-profits were mostly mom-and-pop trade schools. Twenty years ago, a series of high-profile Congressional hearings, led by Senator Sam Nunn, revealed widespread fraud in the industry, and the resulting reforms almost wiped the schools out. But they hung on and returned with a vengeance in the form of publicly traded giants like the University of Phoenix.

Entrepreneurs like Clifford, meanwhile, have been snapping up dying nonprofit colleges and quickly turning them into money-making machines.

Most of that money comes from the federal government, in the form of Pell Grants and subsidized student loans. [The University of] Phoenix alone is on pace to reap $1-billion from Pell Grants this year, along with $4-billion from federal loans. A quarter of all federal aid goes to for-profits, while they enroll only 10 percent of students.

For-Profits on the Hot Seat

Unfortunately, a large and growing number of graduates of for-profit colleges are having trouble paying those loans back. Horror stories of aggressive recruiters' inducing students to take out huge loans for nearly worthless degrees are filling the news. The [Barack] Obama administration, flush with victory after vanquishing the student-loan industry this year [2010], has proposed cutting off federal aid to for-profits that saddle students with unmanageable debt. Congress has rolled out the TV cameras for a new round of hearings that are putting for-profits on the hot seat. One observer called the event "the Nunn hearings on steroids."

The new scrutiny of for-profits is welcome. Without oversight, the combination of government subsidies and financially unsophisticated consumers guarantees outright fraud or programs that, while technically legitimate, are so substandard that the distinction of legitimacy has no meaning. For-profit owners and advocates have a hard time admitting that.

I spoke with Michael Clifford recently as he was driving down the California coast to meet with a higher-education charity he runs. He's an interesting man—sincere, optimistic, a true believer in higher education and his role as a force for good. A musician and born-again Christian, he learned at the knee of the University of Phoenix's founder, John Sperling. In 2004, Clifford led the sale of a destitute Baptist institution called Grand Canyon University to investors. Six years later, enrollment has increased substantially, much of it online. The ownership company started selling shares to the public in 2008 and is worth nearly $1-billion today, making Clifford a wealthy man. He has since repeated the formula elsewhere, partnering with notables like General Electric's former chief executive, Jack Welch. Some of the colleges that Clifford has purchased have given him honorary degrees (thus "Doctor" Michael Clifford).

Clifford will concede, in the abstract, to abuses in the for-profit industry. But he rejects the Obama administration's proposal to cut off federal aid to for-profits at which student-debt payments after graduation exceed a certain percentage of the graduates' income. In fact, he denies that colleges have any responsibility whatsoever for how much students borrow and whether they can pay it back. He won't even acknowledge that student borrowing is related to how much colleges charge.

Profiting on Weaker Students

That refusal is the industry line, and it is crazy nonsense. As a rule, for-profits charge much more than public colleges and universities. Many of their students come from moderate- and low-income backgrounds. You don't need a college degree to know that large debt plus small income equals high risk of default. The for-profit Corinthian Colleges estimated in official documents filed with the Securities and Exchange Commission that more than half the loans it makes to its own students will go bad. Corinthian still makes a profit, because it gets most of its money from loans guaranteed by Uncle Sam.

Other industry officials, like the for-profit lobbyist Harris Miller, would have you believe that government money that technically passes through the hands of students on its way from the public treasury to the for-profit bottom line isn't a government subsidy at all. In that regard, for-profits lately have been trying to rebrand themselves as "market based" higher education. To understand how wrong this is, look no further than the "90/10 rule," a federal rule that bars for-profits from receiving more than 90 percent of their revenue from federal aid. The fact that the rule exists at all, and that Miller is working to water it down (it used to be the 85/15 rule), shows that for-profits operate in nothing like a subsidy-free market.

The federal government has every right to regulate the billions of taxpayer dollars it is pouring into the pockets of for-profit shareholders. The sooner abusive colleges are prevented from loading students with crushing debt in exchange for low-value degrees, the better.

For-Profits Are Innovators

But that doesn't mean for-profit higher education is inherently bad. The reputable parts of the industry are at the forefront of much technological and organizational innovation. For-profits exist in large part to fix educational market failures left by traditional institutions, and they profit by serving students that public and private nonprofit institutions too often ignore. While old-line research universities were gilding their walled-off academic city-states, the University of Phoenix was building no-frills campuses near freeway exits so working students could take classes in the evening. Who was more focused on the public interest? Some of the colleges Clifford bought have legacies that stretch back decades. Who else was willing to save them? Not the government, or the church, or the more fortunate colleges with their wealthy alumni and endowments that reach the sky.

The for-profit Kaplan University recently struck a deal with the California community-college system to provide courses that the bankrupt public colleges cannot. The president of the system's faculty senate objected: The deal was not "favorable to faculty," she said. Whose fault is that? Kaplan, or the feckless voters and incompetent politicians who have driven California to ruin?

Wal-Mart recently announced a deal with the for-profit American Public University to teach the giant retailer's employees. What ambitious president or provost is planning to make her reputation educating $9-an-hour cashiers?

No Objective Measures of Quality

Traditional institutions tend to respond to such ventures by indicting the quality of for-profit degrees. The trouble is, they have very little evidence beyond the real issue of default rates to prove it. That's because traditional institutions have long resisted subjecting themselves to any objective measures of academic

Students move into dorms at the for-profit Grand Canyon University. Started as an investment in 2004, the school is now worth nearly a billion dollars.

quality. They've pointed instead to regional accreditation, which conveniently allows colleges to decide for themselves whether they're doing a good job.

But many for-profit institutions have regional accreditation, too. That's what people like Clifford are buying when they invest in troubled colleges. Accreditation has become like a taxicab medallion, available for bidding on the open market. As a result, long-established public and private nonprofit colleges are left with no standards with which to make the case against their for-profit competitors. At one recent Congressional hearing, the Senate education committee's chairman, Tom Harkin, said of the for-profits, "We don't know how many students graduate, how many get jobs, how schools that are not publicly traded spend their [federal] dollars, and how many for-profit students default over the long term." All true—and just as true when the words "for profit" are removed. There's no doubt that the worst for-profits are ruthlessly exploiting the commodified college degree. But they didn't commodify it in the first place.

For-profits fill a void left by traditional institutions that once believed their world was constant. Fast-developing methods of teaching students over the Internet have given the velocity of change a turbo boost. In such a volatile situation, all kinds of unexpected people make their way into the picture. And once they get there, they tend to stick around. Traditional institutions hoping that Congress will rid them of for-profit competition will very likely be disappointed.

THIRTEEN

The Federal Government Should Increase Support for Community Colleges

Barack Obama

> The following viewpoint was originally a speech given in the summer of 2009 by Barack Obama to introduce a new program, the American Graduation Initiative, to support the work of community colleges. In the new economy, he argues, many of the manufacturing jobs that American workers once held are gone forever, and today's workers must acquire more training to qualify for the jobs that are being created. Community colleges provide solid technological training at an affordable price, he points out, but many of them have out-of-date facilities and more applicants than they can serve. Federal support for community colleges, he concludes, will help the nation prosper.
>
> Obama is the forty-fourth president of the United States of America.

Now, [Macomb Community College in Michigan] is a place where anyone—anyone with a desire to learn and to grow, to take their career to a new level or start a new career altogether—has the opportunity to pursue their dream, right here in Macomb. This is a place where people of all ages and all backgrounds—even

Barack Obama, "Remarks by the President on the American Graduation Initiative, Macomb Community College, Warren, Michigan," whitehouse.gov, July 14, 2009.

in the face of obstacles, even in the face of very difficult personal challenges—can take a chance on a brighter future for themselves and their families. . . .

There are workers like Kellie Kulman, who is here today. Kellie is a UAW [United Auto Workers] worker at a Ford plant in Sterling Heights, Michigan. She used to drive a fork lift, right? But then she decided to train here at Macomb for a job that required new skills, and now she's an apprentice pipe fitter. It's a telling example: Even as this painful restructuring takes place in our auto industry, workers are seeking out training for new auto jobs. And Kellie's story makes clear what all of you know: Community colleges are an essential part of our recovery in the present—and our prosperity in the future. This place can make the future better, not just for these individuals but for America. . . .

Now, my administration has a job to do, as well, and that job is to get this economy back on its feet. That's my job. And it's a job I gladly accept. I love these folks who helped get us in this mess and then suddenly say, well, this is Obama's economy. That's fine. Give it to me. My job is to solve problems, not to stand on the sidelines and harp and gripe. . . .

New Jobs for a New Economy

The hard truth is, is that some of the jobs that have been lost in the auto industry and elsewhere won't be coming back. They're the casualties of a changing economy. In some cases, just increased productivity in the plants themselves means that some jobs aren't going to return. And that only underscores the importance of generating new businesses and new industries to replace the ones that we've lost, and of preparing our workers to fill the jobs they create. For even before this recession hit, we were faced with an economy that was simply not creating or sustaining enough new, well-paying jobs. . . .

But we also have to ensure that we're educating and preparing our people for the new jobs of the 21st century. We've got to prepare our people with the skills they need to compete in this global economy. Time and again, when we placed our bet for the future on education, we have prospered as a result—by tapping the incredible innovative and generative potential of a skilled American workforce. That's what happened when President [Abraham] Lincoln signed into law legislation creating the land grant colleges, which not only transformed higher education, but also our entire economy. That's what took place when President [Franklin D.] Roosevelt signed the GI Bill which helped educate a generation, and ushered in an era of unprecedented prosperity. That was the foundation for the American middle class.

And that's why, at the start of my administration I set a goal for America: By 2020, this nation will once again have the highest proportion of college graduates in the world. We used to have that. We're going to have it again. And we've begun to take historic steps to achieve this goal. Already we've increased Pell grants by $500. We've created a $2,500 tax credit for four years of college tuition. We've simplified student aid applications and ensured that aid is not based on the income of a job that you just lost. A new GI Bill of Rights for the 21st century is beginning to help soldiers coming home from Iraq and Afghanistan to begin a new life—in a new economy. And the recovery plan has helped close state budget shortfalls—which put enormous pressure on public universities and community colleges—at the same time making historic investments in school libraries and classrooms and facilities all across America. So we've already taken some steps that are building the foundation for a 21st century education system here in America, one that will allow us to compete with China and India and everybody else all around the world.

Five Million Degrees and Certificates

But today I'm announcing the most significant down payment yet on reaching the goal of having the highest college graduation rate of any nation in the world. We're going to achieve this in the next 10 years. And it's called the American Graduation Initiative. It will reform and strengthen community colleges like this one from coast to coast so they get the resources that students and schools

President Barack Obama speaks at Michigan's Macomb Community College on July 14, 2009, about his proposal for a multibillion-dollar investment in the nation's community colleges.

need—and the results workers and businesses demand. Through this plan, we seek to help an additional 5 million Americans earn degrees and certificates in the next decade—5 million. . . .

Now, I know that for a long time there have been politicians who have spoken of training as a silver bullet and college as a cure-all. It's not, and we know that. I can't tell you how many workers who've been laid off, you talk to them about training and they say, "Training for what?" So I understand the frustrations that a lot of people have, especially if the training is not well designed for the specific jobs that are being created out there.

But we know that in the coming years, jobs requiring at least an associate degree are projected to grow twice as fast as jobs requiring no college experience. We will not fill those jobs—or even keep those jobs here in America—without the training offered by community colleges. That's why I want to applaud Governor [Jennifer] Granholm for the No Worker Left Behind program. It's providing up to two years' worth of free tuition at community colleges and universities across the state. The rest of the country should learn from the effort.

This is training to become a medical technician, or a health IT [information technology] worker, or a lab specialist, or a nurse. In fact, 59 percent of all new nurses come from community colleges. This is training to install solar panels and build those wind turbines we were talking about and develop a smarter electricity grid. And this is the kind of education that more and more Americans are using to improve their skills and broaden their horizons. Many young people are saving money by spending two years at community college before heading to a four-year college. And more workers who have lost their jobs—or fear losing a job—are seeking an edge at schools like this one.

At the same time, community colleges are under increasing pressure to cap enrollments and scrap courses and cut costs as states and municipalities face budget shortfalls. And this is in addition to the challenges you face in the best of times, as these schools receive far less funding per student than typical four-year colleges and universities. So community colleges are an undervalued asset in our country. Not only is that not right, it's not smart. That's why I've asked Dr. Jill Biden—who happens to be a relation [the wife] of the Vice President, Joe Biden, but who is also a community college educator for more than 16 years—to promote community colleges and help us make community colleges stronger. And that's why we're putting in place this American Graduation Initiative.

Funding for Innovation

Let me describe for you the specifics of what we're going to do. Number one, we will offer competitive grants, challenging community colleges to pursue innovative, results-oriented strategies in exchange for federal funding. We'll fund programs that connect students looking for jobs with businesses that are looking to hire. We'll challenge these schools to find new and better ways to help students catch up on the basics, like math and science, that are essential to our competitiveness. We'll put colleges and employers together to create programs that match curricula in the classroom with the needs of the boardroom. . . .

In addition, we want to propose new funding for innovative strategies that promote not just enrollment in a community college program, but completion of that program. See, more than half of all students who enter community college to earn an associate degree, or transfer to a four-year school to earn a bachelor's degree, unfortunately fail to reach their goal. That's not just a waste of a valuable resource, that's a tragedy for these students. Oftentimes they've taken out debt and they don't get the degree, but they still have to pay back the debt. And it's a disaster for our economy.

So we'll fund programs that track student progress inside and outside the classroom. Let's figure out what's keeping students from crossing that finish line, and then put in place reforms that will remove those barriers. Maybe it becomes too difficult for a parent to be away from home, or too expensive for a waiter or a nurse to miss a shift. Maybe a young student just isn't sure if her education will lead to employment. The point is, we need to figure out solutions for these kinds of challenges—because facing these impediments shouldn't prevent you from reaching your potential.

Facilities: Real and Virtual

All right, so that's a big chunk of this first part of this initiative. The second part: We're going to back $10 billion in loans to renovate and rebuild college classrooms and buildings all across the country. All too often, community colleges are treated like the stepchild of the higher education system; they're an afterthought, if they're thought of at all. And that means schools are often years behind in the facilities they provide, which means, in a 21st century economy, they're years behind in the education they can offer. That's a mistake and it's one that we'll help to correct. Through this fund, schools will have the chance to borrow at a more affordable rate to modernize facilities, and they'll be building on the funds in the recovery plan that are already helping to renovate schools, including community colleges all across the country. And by the way, not only does this improve the schools and the training that they're providing, [but] guess what? You also

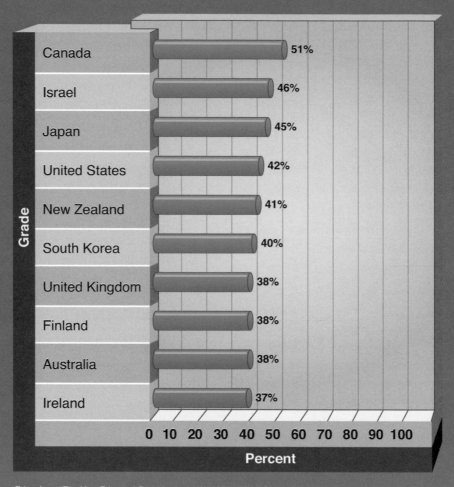

Most-Educated Countries

The United States ranks fourth in the percentage of its population holding a college degree or equivalent.

Grade	Percent
Canada	51%
Israel	46%
Japan	45%
United States	42%
New Zealand	41%
South Korea	40%
United Kingdom	38%
Finland	38%
Australia	38%
Ireland	37%

0 10 20 30 40 50 60 70 80 90 100

Percent

Taken from: "The Most Educated Countries in the World." 24/7 Wall Street, September 21, 2012. http://247wallst.com.

have to hire some workers and some tradesmen and women to do the work on those schools. So it means it's putting people to work in Michigan right here right now.

Number three: Even as we repair bricks and mortar, we have an opportunity to build a new virtual infrastructure to complement the education and training community colleges can offer. So we're going to support the creation of a new online, open-source clearinghouse of courses so that community colleges across the country can offer more classes without building more classrooms. And this will make a big difference especially for rural campuses that a lot of times have to struggle to attract students and faculty. And this will make it possible for a professor to complement his lecture with an online exercise, or for a student who can't be away from her family to still keep up with her coursework. We don't know where this kind of experiment will lead, but that's exactly why we ought to try it because I think there's a possibility that online education can provide especially for people who are already in the workforce and want to retrain the chance to upgrade their skills without having to quit their job.

So let me say this once more: The road to recovery, the road to prosperity, is going to be hard. . . .

And it's going to take time. There are going to be false starts and there are going to be setbacks. But I am confident that we can meet the challenges we face, because that's what we've always done. That's what America does. We hit some challenges, we fuss and argue about it, and then we go ahead and go about the business of solving our problems. That's what we see on display right here at Macomb Community College. That's what I've seen at colleges and universities all across this country. At every juncture in our history when we've been challenged, we have summoned the resilience and the industriousness—that can-do American spirit—that has allowed us to succeed in the face of even the toughest odds.

That's what we can and must do now, not just to overcome this crisis, but to leave something better behind, to lay a foundation on which our children and our grandchildren can prosper and take responsibility for their future—just as the students at this school, at this difficult moment, are taking responsibility for theirs.

FOURTEEN

Germany's Career-Focused Education System Reduces Unemployment

Edward Lotterman

In the following viewpoint Edward Lotterman argues that the US education model, in which most students follow the same path from kindergarten through twelfth grade, does not serve many students well. Germany's model, he points out, allows students to begin following a career track and gain workplace experience as early as age fourteen. While the American model was originally intended to give equal opportunity for social mobility to all students, today it is harder than ever for low-income young people to rise out of poverty, he contends. Americans should closely examine the educational system, he concludes, and consider borrowing successful ideas from Germany.

Lotterman is a professor of economics at Augsburg College in Minneapolis and writes a blog called *Real World Economics*.

At a time of 8.2 percent unemployment and millions out of work in the U.S., how could an estimated 600,000 highly placed technical jobs remain unfilled for lack of qualified applicants? The answer may lie in the changing structure and expectations of the American educational system.

Simply put: Are we properly training our young people to participate in today's economy?

Different countries have different methods of training people for technical jobs. Here in the United States, the model is one of all students pursuing a basically similar curriculum from kindergarten through 12th grade.

At that point, graduates join the full-time workforce or go on to some sort of "postsecondary" institution. The most common ones are colleges and universities for people going into white-collar careers and vocational-technical schools for those who will do skilled work with their hands.

In Germany, students face a fork in the road at about age 14. Many continue on an academic track that prepares them for entry into a university; others take a vocational branch that will combine classroom study with workplace apprenticeship training. This track applies not only to those headed into manufacturing and skilled trades, but also service-sector and retail jobs. Nearly 400 separate occupational titles have apprentice programs tailored for them.

Each system has advantages and disadvantages. Each reflects the history and culture of the nation using it.

Loyal and Highly Skilled Technicians

Germany is an orderly nation that values continuity. Its apprenticeship system links directly back to the guild system of the middle ages. This system continued forward through the nation's unification and dramatic industrialization in the 1800s and, in remarkably similar formats, through 45 years of separation into free-market West and communist East.

Moreover, in addition to world-scale industrial conglomerates like Krupp, Siemens and Volkswagen, the German economy and its status as a world exporter have always depended on myriad medium-size firms, often family-owned and managed for generations, that produce specialized machinery of all types.

The apprenticeship system is inextricably linked with these "*mittelstand*" [small- and medium-size] firms, producing highly skilled technicians with great loyalty to specific companies and with expertise that allows as many innovations to come up from the shop floor as from the offices of engineers with university degrees.

But the German system inherently involves making near-irrevocable decisions about a person's life career at an early age, when young people's preferences and true abilities are imperfectly formed or measurable.

This is not unique. Nearly all European education systems long incorporated nodal points at which an ever-decreasing elite continued through to training for upper-class careers while less smart, or less favored, students were shunted aside toward unskilled or skilled manual labor. In most cases, these nodes centered around high-pressure written exams.

Opportunity for All

Americans correctly saw this European approach as perpetuating a class system in which the children of upper-class and middle-class parents moved briskly along paths that would maintain their privileged status while the children of manual workers were herded through chutes to replace their parents in a coal mine shaft or on a mill floor.

Better, Americans argued, to afford the same opportunities to all, so that anyone who completed high school could have an equal shot at colleges, universities and an "American dream" career track. Those who chose not to go to college could go directly to work with a good background in reading, writing, math and science that would stand them well in many workplaces or prepare them for vocational education as needed.

Yes, apprenticeship programs like those in Germany turned out battalions of superb craftsmen. But here in the U.S., we also had millions of workers who became skilled machinists, welders, die

Apprentices check an engine at a Porsche plant in Leipzig, Germany. Germany's apprentice programs produce highly skilled technicians who have great loyalty to the companies that train them.

makers and so forth. Moreover, many of them, including [auto company founders] Henry Ford, Walter P. Chrysler and Samuel Vauclain (of Baldwin Locomotive fame) eventually went from laboring at a vise with a file in hand to running the largest corporations in the world.

For decades, the American critique was true. Social mobility was lower in Europe than in our own country, and European schooling, including apprenticeship programs, contributed to that.

Trapped by the System of Education

However, now (and most Americans ignore this fact), social mobility in the United States is markedly lower than it was in the past and lower than in nearly any EU [European Union] nation. And now, many argue, the trappings of U.S. egalitarian schooling serve to perpetuate social class rigidities. It has never been so true that if your parents went to college, you are highly likely to, and if they did not, you probably won't.

And if you don't go on after high school, you nearly certainly won't be qualified for one of some 600,000 good-paying technical jobs that stand unfilled right now for lack of qualified applicants.

We in the U.S. blame low-wage East Asian exporters like China for the demise of U.S. manufacturing employment. Many also fault U.S. labor unions. But Germany, whose manufacturing workers average higher earnings than their U.S. counterparts with equivalent technical skills, continues as the world's second largest

The Skills Gap

In a 2012 survey of small business CEOs, 31 percent identified being "unable to identify applicants with the appropriate experience or skills" as the primary reasons they had unfilled jobs.

31%
Unable to identify applicants with the
appropriate experience or skills

Taken from: *The Wall Street Journal*/Vistage Small Business CEO survey, July 2012. http://online.wsj.com.

exporter. With only 82 million people, it exports only slightly less than China, which has 1.334 billion people.

Yes, there are many other factors, including Germany's favorable position within the EU and the euro currency system.

The fact is, however, that an educational system once vaunted as providing opportunity for lower-class people now not only traps them in their status, but channels many into lives of economic marginality at best, and of crime at worst. We should be able to do better.

FIFTEEN

High School Students Should Have More Opportunities for Workplace Experience

Dana Goldstein

In the following viewpoint Dana Goldstein interviews education consultant Nancy Hoffman about the current focus in the United States on preparing young people for careers after they have finished high school instead of beginning their occupational training sooner. Switzerland provides a model, Hoffman argues, of a successful system that encourages teens as young as sixteen to earn school credit for on-the-job work experience. She concludes that people in the United States need to adjust their attitudes about the capabilities of young people and the value of career and technical education and be willing to follow successful European examples.

Goldstein is an award-winning journalist who focuses on education, women's issues, public health, and American politics.

Dana Goldstein, "The Future of Vocational Education." Reprinted with permission from the April 19, 2012 issue of *The Nation*. For subscription information, call 1-800-333-8536. Portions of each week's Nation magazine can be accessed at http://www.thenation.com.

In Iowa today [April 19, 2012], Secretary of Education Arne Duncan unveiled the [Barack] Obama administration's new vocational education plan. The president proposes to revise the Carl D. Perkins Career and Technical Education Act by investing an additional $1 billion to increase partnerships between high schools, colleges and employers, with the goal of directing students toward high-need industries such as engineering and healthcare.

But the choice of venue for the announcement—the Des Moines Area Community College—underscores a critique of the president's education and jobs agenda aired on both the right and left: that it focuses too much on post-high school occupational training, and not enough on introducing younger adolescents to the world of work outside the classroom. Indeed, the administration's policy blueprint states that high school students enrolled in career and technical education programs must still achieve "mastery of the core academic content required of all students." In many Western European nations, on the other hand, the high school curriculum is significantly differentiated for teenagers depending on whether they are headed to a liberal arts university, a technical college, or into the workforce.

In a new book, *Schooling in the Workplace*, Nancy Hoffman of Jobs for the Future argues the United States should adopt a Swiss-style vocational education system, in which students in their last two years of high school have the option of participating in highly structured workplace apprenticeships, working for pay several days per week and spending the rest of the time in the classroom. "We have a 22 percent youth unemployment rate right now, compared to 5 percent in the Netherlands or Switzerland," Hoffman told *The Nation*. "Among that 22 percent are young people who are going to be permanently scarred, and that's damaging to the human psyche. We don't think about what we can do to help the young people in our charge discover the role of work in our lives."

In the following interview, I talk with Hoffman about why vocational education is so controversial in the United States, what role the liberal arts should play and how emphasizing career training might change the teaching profession. The interview has been condensed and edited for clarity.

Dana Goldstein: I was fascinated by your idea of providing older teens—especially "the forgotten half" that will not attend a four-year college—with an easier "transition to adulthood." You describe upper secondary school students in Switzerland working behind the counter in a cell phone shop for school credit, which will certainly horrify a lot of advocates of a college-prep curriculum. Can you talk about why you think this type of "transitional" work is so important?

Nancy Hoffman: In Switzerland there are whole stores run by kids, so there are multiple jobs including management, repair, all the technical jobs, plus customer service. If we have a situation in the United States where only about 20 percent of 26-year-olds have any credential, we need something for people to do to get them from 16 to 20 without landing in jail, on welfare or on the street; something that gives them a structure and lets them figure out their potential and interests.

This guy working in customer service at the cell phone shop was going to get a retail certificate in meeting the national standard. And whether he is going to make the leap forward to become a cell phone designer, who knows? But being in a setting where adults have goals, having a structure from age 16 to 19, seems like a much more positive option than what many young adults experience in our country. This Swiss person has an income. He gets paid anywhere from 800 to 1,000 euros per month. He has to demonstrate his competencies in sales. He will have the equivalent of really a year or two of community college, because he was also going to school two days per week.

What about students learning how to debate the big ideas in literature and in politics? What about gaining exposure to great art and writing about it?

In the United States, we need a much stronger set of academic demands up to age 16. But for the large mass of young people who are muddling along between 16 and 22, trying not to land in jail, or be unemployed or on the street—or even just going from job to job—you might have to ask: What would be a good enough system? And we know people who pay taxes and have jobs and have healthcare are much more likely to vote, to use social services and to participate in democracy. As for the debate of the big ideas, the number of students who actually get to do that is relatively small. I don't like the idea of giving it up, but it's probably unfortunately very much class-based in this country anyhow.

You really like the Swiss system. What one or two aspects of it do you think are most realistic for American states to implement?

Volkswagen is starting a European-style apprenticeship program in Tennessee, but for high school graduates. The first thing that has to happen is employers have to be able to see there is some self-interest in engaging with young people in the workplace. That's a very tough sell. You probably have to start with more internships and apprenticeships at the community college level than in high school, because most people in this country just don't believe that 16-year-olds can be productive workers—though there is plenty of evidence they certainly can be.

The second thing, which is maybe boring but most important, is the combination of employer and government infrastructure to support employers in taking in young people. I was just in North Carolina talking about this stuff with business leaders, and they really sort of got it. The Swiss government particularly invests a great deal in analysis of jobs to figure out what competencies should exist. They invest in initial workplace training [for apprenticeship hosts], because small businesses can't do this on their own. It's a whole intermediary infrastructure, plus a research and support structure shared between employers and the government, which makes this possible. There are just a few institutions or non-profits, like workforce investment boards, that do this in the United States.

You are a fan of "dual systems" in which students learn theoretical subjects in school, say two days per week, and more practical

"There's an apprenticeship opportunity on TV tonight." Cartoon by Grizelda. www.Cartoon Stock.com.

ones in the workplace three days per week. But does emphasizing practical learning, as the German and Swiss systems do, make academic high school teaching a less prestigious or desirable profession? Making teaching more elite is a major goal of American education reform, and it seems like de-emphasizing the traditional classroom *might have certain adverse effects on teaching that your book doesn't acknowledge.*

I get where you're coming from, because you're coming from a U.S. context. But this is not even a question in the European countries. In Finland, as you know, there are ten applicants for every place in teachers' college, and that's whether you teach in a vocational or an academic program.

It's actually harder to recruit teachers for vocational systems than for academic ones. Except in a few countries with really highly regarded systems, "vocational" still carries a stigma. And despite all the good things I say about the vocational system, I only know a couple of families in Europe [among my social and professional peers] who sent their kids to the vocational system. Their kids become economists, say, like they are.

Isn't that somewhat disturbing, because it suggests the vocational track really is the track for working-class kids?

It's not disturbing at all. Income inequality is much greater in the United States than in European countries. There is much greater mobility in the European countries than here. Secondly, my view is that I would much rather have a 3 percent youth unemployment rate and most young people having a job, than have the bifurcated system we have in the United States, [in which some kids go to four-year college, and the rest face a 22 percent unemployment rate].

The really strong countries have pathways from vocational education straight through to technical colleges. An interesting data point from Switzerland is that 42 percent of the students who get fours or fives on PISA [Programme for International Student Assessment] exams [the highest scores] enter the vocational system. That's because they know that if you want to be an engineer, work in IT [information technology] or any of these high-tech jobs, you're going to be much more likely to get a job after real work experience. In Norway, one young woman I met did a university degree in graphic design and then discovered she wanted to go back and do a vocational program, because she needed work experience.

We behave as though nobody needs to learn to work. We behave as if somehow education alone will launch you into a career, although we know almost everyone is going to two- or four-year colleges because they want to get a job. So why one would think that between 16 and 19 years old it isn't good to get some work experience, I don't know.

What You Should Know About Career and Technical Education

Opinions About Postsecondary Education

According to surveys conducted by the Pew Research Center in 2011:

- When asked whether finding a job was easier or harder for today's young people than it was for their parents, 82 percent said finding a job is harder; 12 percent said it is about the same; and 5 percent said it is easier.
- Adults were asked to identify various qualities that are "extremely important in helping a young person succeed in the world today." A good work ethic was identified by 61 percent of respondents; knowing how to get along with people, by 57 percent; work skills learned on the job, by 43 percent; and a college education, by only 42 percent.
- Ninety-four percent of American parents expect their child to go to college.
- When asked whether college is affordable, 75 percent of respondents said that most people cannot afford to pay for a college education, while 22 percent said that college was affordable for most people. In 1985, 39 percent of those surveyed believed that a college education was affordable for most people.

- In a group of adults from various educational backgrounds, 50 percent reported that they were "very satisfied" with their education; 32 percent were "somewhat satisfied"; 10 percent were "somewhat dissatisfied"; and 5 percent were "very dissatisfied."

Training and Jobs

According to February 2012 data from the Bureau of Labor Statistics, the ten occupations projected to grow the fastest between 2010 and 2020 are:

- personal care aides
- home health aides
- biomedical engineers
- helpers—brickmasons, blockmasons, stonemasons, and tile and marble setters
- helpers—carpenters
- veterinary technologists and technicians
- reinforcing iron and rebar workers
- physical therapist assistants
- helpers—pipelayers, plumbers, pipefitters, and steamfitters
- meeting, convention, and event planners

According to 2009 data from the US Census Bureau's American Community Survey:

- Forty percent of adults aged twenty-five to sixty-four held high school diplomas or less; 31 percent had completed some college, including two-year degrees; 19 percent had earned bachelor's degrees; and 11 percent held advanced degrees.

Reporting on Americans aged twenty-five or older who had jobs in September 2012, the Bureau of Labor Statistics stated that:

- the largest group, 37.2 percent, held bachelor's degrees or higher, 28.1 percent had completed some college or an associate's degree, 26.7 percent had competed high school, and 7.9 percent had less than a high school diploma; and

- employment among those with at least an associate's degree increased by approximately 578,000 between April and September 2012, while the number of jobs held by those with only a high school diploma has not increased since 2010.

The Partnership for 21st Century Skills recognizes the value of the traditional three R's of education (reading, writing, and arithmetic), and urges educational programs to also emphasize new "learning and innovation skills"—the "four C's":

- critical thinking
- communication
- collaboration
- creativity

USA Today reported in October 2012 that:

- the manufacturing sector in the United States had created five hundred thousand new jobs in the two previous years;
- in a survey conducted by the Manufacturing Institute, 82 percent of those responding said that they would like to create more manufacturing jobs, but that they knew that qualified applicants were not available, while 80 percent expected that the lack of qualified candidates will not be remedied in the near future.

A consortium of business training professional organizations issued a research report, The Ill-Prepared U.S. Workforce, in 2009. They found that when employers were asked to evaluate how well prepared new employees were to do their jobs, the employers' replies included the following:

- Employers hiring workers with only high school diplomas rated the preparation of 33.9 percent of their new hires as "deficient"; 50.6 percent were rated "adequate"; and 15.6 percent were rated "excellent."
- Employers hiring workers with associate's degrees rated the preparation of 21.7 percent of their new hires "deficient"; 54.6 percent "adequate"; and 23.7 percent "excellent."

- Employers hiring workers with bachelor's degrees rated the preparation of 17.4 percent of their new hires "deficient"; 51.1 percent "adequate"; and 31.5 percent "excellent."

Students taking classes at eleven high-school-level technology centers were asked by the Southern Regional Education Board about their studies. Slightly less than half—48 percent—reported that they took challenging courses in high school. Their top four reasons, according to a 2012 report:

- They will prepare me for my goal(s) beyond high school.
- I like being challenged.
- My teachers or counselors encouraged me to take them.
- My parents encouraged me to take them.

In the same study, 52 percent of the students said that they had not taken challenging courses in high school. Their top four reasons:

- They are not necessary for my goal(s) beyond high school.
- They are too difficult.
- Nobody encouraged me to take them.
- I do not understand the point of taking such courses.

Career and Technical Education

According to the National Association of State Directors of Career Technical Education Consortium:

- Approximately 14 million students are enrolled in career and technical education (CTE) programs in US high schools and two-year colleges.
- High school students enrolled in CTE programs graduate at a higher rate—90.2 percent—than their peers. The national average of high school freshmen who persist to graduation is 74.9 percent.
- Students who concentrate in CTE programs in high school are more likely than their peers to attend college and to remain in college through graduation.

- Of the 47 million job openings projected for the decade ending in 2018, about a third will require an associate's degree or a certificate.
- Data studied in 2012 show that there are 29 million jobs in the United States that pay middle-class wages yet require less than a four-year degree. Most of these jobs have qualifications that can be met with certificates and associate's degrees.

What You Should Do About Career and Technical Education

Because career and technical education is such a wide and rapidly changing field, the most important thing to do about it is learn what you can. As the world economy changes and global markets shift, the job market also shifts, and many twenty-first-century jobs—most of which require some education beyond a high school diploma—call for new skills and new kinds of training. There are literally thousands of colleges, universities, technical schools, and career academies in the United States, and finding those that best suit your interests and your goals can be challenging. Fortunately, many high schools have counselors on staff who help students find the right schools and programs for them; public libraries have materials to help people research jobs and schools; and the Internet offers many websites—sponsored by schools, professional organizations and government agencies, as well as by companies that charge fees to help you find answers—with invaluable information.

Choosing a Career Path

A good place to start is the *Occupational Outlook Handbook (OOH)*, a career guide published every two years by the federal Bureau of Labor Statistics (BLS), describing hundreds of occupations. For each one, the *OOH* describes what workers do on the job; what the work environment is like, including any special physical or emotional demands, typical work schedules, and possible hazards workers face; the education, training and other qualifications needed to enter the occupation, including information about certificates and licenses required; the money and benefits a typical worker in this occupation can expect to earn; and whether demand for these workers is expected to expand or shrink in the coming years. Finally, the book gives contact information for other organizations and agencies to help you find out more about a particular job.

The *Occupational Outlook Handbook* is published in a print version, probably available at your local public library, as well as online (www.bls.gov/ooh/ or www.bls.gov/ooh/mobile). The BLS sponsors a special website geared to students who have not yet graduated from high school. Called "What Do You Like?" (www.bls.gov/k12/index.htm), it is designed to help students explore careers by first considering their own interests.

Other ways to learn about careers include talking with counselors and teachers at your school and interviewing people who do the kind of work you might like to do. Reading job postings in newspapers and magazines, or those posted online at your state's job bank, will help you see what kinds of qualifications and experience employers are looking for. Many schools and communities host job fairs, bringing employers and potential employees together. As you narrow down your choice of careers or your list of institutions where you might seek additional training, you will find that most colleges, universities, and technical and career schools have placement counselors and career counselors who will help you decide whether your goals are realistic and a good match for you and will help you make a plan for preparing for your chosen occupation.

Getting the Education and Training You Need

If you are not ready to commit to a four-year college degree program, or if your career plans do not require a four-year degree, there are many options available to find training and education for a good job. Many high schools provide career and technical education (CTE) programs that students enroll in while they are still in high school, offering them the opportunity to explore career options before high school graduation. (If your high school does not offer such programs, check out other local high schools, that may offer them.) In these programs, which provide students with academic knowledge and technical skills, you will start to get "real world" education in fields that include manufacturing, agriculture, health sciences, and technology. When you finish high school, you'll be ready for the next step: either a job or further education and training.

There are many institutions that offer career and technical training, and what may seem an overwhelming number of questions to ask about them: Will you need just a few courses, a professional certificate, or a two- or four-year degree? Should you attend a public nonprofit institution or a private for-profit institution? Should you go full-time or part-time? Might you be able to complete your studies online? If you decide to continue on for a four-year degree, are your courses likely to transfer to another institution? Who accredits the institution?

Online courses and programs are a relatively new addition to the educational landscape. If you will be working while you go to school, or if you have child care or other responsibilities, online courses can give you more flexibility to schedule your schoolwork around your other duties. But online courses are not for everyone. You must be comfortable working with a computer and have reliable access to a computer and the Internet, and you must be self-motivated enough to do your schoolwork independently without daily reminders or regular class meetings. If you are not sure whether online courses would be a good fit for you, try taking the quiz posted by the Minnesota State Colleges and Universities (www.minnesotaonline.org/students/distancelearningquiz.php). The good news is that the US Department of Education determined in a 2009 study that students who take their online education seriously and follow through with course requirements do as well or better than students who take traditional courses.

Several publications and websites can help you choose a program after you finish high school. The most well-known organization gathering and distributing information about colleges is Peterson's (www.petersons.com). Its website can help walk you through the process of choosing a school and includes information about four-year colleges and universities, community colleges, and public and private vocational and technical schools. Again, if your high school staff includes a college or career counselor, your first step should be to schedule an appointment to discuss your plans—and ask your questions—face-to-face.

The editors have compiled the following list of organizations concerned with the issues debated in this book. The descriptions are derived from materials provided by the organizations. All have publications or information available for interested readers. The list was compiled on the date of publication of the present volume; names, addresses, phone and fax numbers, and e-mail and Internet addresses may change. Be aware that many organizations take several weeks or longer to respond to inquiries, so allow as much time as possible.

Alliance for Excellent Education
1201 Connecticut Ave. NW, Ste. 901
Washington, DC 20036
(202) 828-0828
website: www.all4ed.org/

The Alliance for Excellent Education is a national policy and advocacy organization that works to improve national policy so that all students can achieve at high academic levels and graduate from high school ready for success in college, work, and citizenship in the twenty-first century. The alliance focuses on America's 6 million most at-risk secondary school students—those in the lowest achievement quartile—who are most likely to leave school without a diploma or to graduate unprepared for a productive future. The website includes a blog, a resource library, and a section on career and technical education, with fact sheets and reports, including "A Framework for Advancing Career and Technical Education: Recommendations for the Reauthorization of the Carl D. Perkins Act" and "Preparing Students for College and Career: California Multiple Pathways."

American Association of Community Colleges (AACC)
One Dupont Circle NW, Ste. 410
Washington, DC 20036

(202) 728-0200
fax: (202) 833-2467
website: www.aacc.nche.edu

The AACC is the primary advocacy organization for the nation's community colleges. The association represents nearly twelve hundred two-year, associate's degree–granting institutions and more than 13 million students. AACC promotes community colleges through five strategic action areas: (1) recognition and advocacy for community colleges; (2) student access, learning, and success; (3) community college leadership development; (4) economic and workforce development; and (5) global and intercultural education. Among the "Hot Issues" featured on its website are Economic/Workforce Development, Sustainability/Green Jobs, and Technology. The site also offers reports, white papers, and research and project briefs, including "Just How Similar? Community Colleges and the For-Profit Sector" and "Doing More with Less: The Inequitable Funding of Community Colleges."

Association for Career and Technical Education (ACTE)
1410 King St.
Alexandria, VA 22314
(800) 826-9972
fax: (703) 683-7424
website: www.acteonline.org

Founded in 1926, the ACTE is the largest national education association dedicated to the advancement of education that prepares youth and adults for successful careers. The strength of ACTE is reflected in its diverse membership, composed of more than twenty-seven thousand career and technical educators, administrators, researchers, guidance counselors, and others involved in planning and conducting career and technical education programs at the secondary, postsecondary, and adult levels. ACTE publishes the *CTE Policy Watch* blog, and the website includes issue briefs such as "CTE's Role in Urban Education," "CTE's Role in Worker Retraining," and "CTE's Role in Adolescent Literacy."

Association of Private-Sector Colleges and Universities (APSCU)
1101 Connecticut Ave. NW, Ste. 900
Washington, DC 20036
(202) 336-6700
fax: (202) 336-6828
website: www.career.org

APSCU is a membership organization of accredited, private, postsecondary schools, institutes, colleges, and universities that provide career-specific educational programs. APSCU has over eighteen hundred members that educate and support almost 2 million students each year for employment in over two hundred occupational fields. APSCU is the premier source of crucial information and public policy recommendations that promote access to career education and the importance of workforce development. The website includes newsletters and reports, a "Compliance and Ethics" library of policies and presentations, and a student spotlight.

Community College Research Center (CCRC)
Teachers College, Columbia University
439 Thorndike Hall
525 W. 120th St., Box 174
New York, NY 10027
(212) 678-3091
fax: (212) 678-3699
e-mail: ccrc@columbia.edu
website: http:// ccrc.tc.columbia.edu

The CCRC is the leading independent authority on the nation's nearly twelve hundred two-year colleges. Its mission is to conduct research on the major issues affecting community colleges in the United States and to contribute to the development of practice and policy that expands access to higher education and promotes success for all students. The website archives dozens of research documents, including the speech "Using Dual Enrollment to Enhance Academic and CTE Pathways" and the

PowerPoint presentation "Building Bridges to CTE for Basic Skills Students."

Jobs for the Future (JFF)
88 Broad St., 8th Fl.
Boston, MA 02110
(617) 728-4446
fax: (617) 728-4857
e-mail: info@jff.org
website: www.jff.org

JFF identifies, develops, and promotes new education and work-force strategies that help communities, states, and the nation compete in a global economy. Jobs for the Future works in the high school and college settings and in the workforce to create strategies and develop schools that will challenge out-of-school youth to receive their diplomas and learn various college preparation skills. JFF publishes research reports, tools, newsletters, and policy briefs that offer insight on education reform and workforce development at local, state, and federal levels. Titles from 2012 include "Innovations in Labor Market Information and Their Application," "An Examination of the Information Technology Job Market," and "Better Care, Better Careers: The Jobs to Careers Strategy for Growing a Skilled Health Care Workforce."

MDRC
16 E. Thirty-Fourth St., 19th Fl.
New York, NY 10016-4326
(212) 532-3200
fax: (212) 684-0832
e-mail: information@mdrc.org
website: www.mdrc.org

Created in 1974 by the Ford Foundation and a group of federal agencies, the nonprofit, nonpartisan organization MDRC is best known for mounting large-scale evaluations of real-world policies and programs targeted at low-income people. The main policy areas in which MDRC works include improving public education, promoting successful transitions to adulthood, supporting low-wage workers and communities, and overcoming barriers to employment. MDRC's research has frequently helped to shape legislation, program design, and operational practices across the country. Policy briefs on the website include "Preparing High School Students for Successful Transitions to Postsecondary Education and Employment" and "Striking the Balance: Career Academies Combine Academic Rigor and Workplace Relevance."

National Association of State Directors of Career Technical Education Consortium (NASDCTEc)
8484 Georgia Ave., Ste. 320
Silver Spring, MD 20910
(301) 588-9630
fax: (301) 588-9631
e-mail: resources@careertech.org
website: www.careertech.org

The NASDCTEc was established in 1920 to represent the state and territory heads of secondary, postsecondary, and adult career technical education (CTE) across the nation. NASDCTEc, through leadership, advocacy and partnerships, aims to support an innovative CTE system that prepares individuals to succeed in education and in their careers and poises the United States to flourish in a dynamic global economy. The website offers issue briefs and papers, webinars and videos, advocacy tools and data snapshots for every state.

National Center for Education Statistics (NCES)
Institute of Education Sciences
1990 K St. NW, Rm. 9061
Washington, DC 20006
website: http://nces.ed.gov

NCES is the primary federal entity for collecting and analyzing data related to education in the United States and other nations. NCES is located within the US Department of Education and the Institute of Education Sciences. NCES maintains a dedicated Career/Technical Education (CTE) Statistics system that uses data from high school transcripts as well as from NCES' surveys of postsecondary students, secondary and postsecondary faculty, and adult learners. NCES has published several reports on career/technical education topics, including "Career and Technical Education in the United States, 1990–2005," the most recent NCES publication that synthesizes career/technical education data at the secondary and postsecondary levels. In addition, the CTE Statistics system is a primary data source for congressionally mandated evaluations of career/technical education.

National Research Center for Career and Technical Education (NRCCTE)
University of Louisville
College of Education and Human Development
Louisville, KY 40292
(502) 852-4727; toll-free: (877) 372-2283
fax: (502) 852-3308
e-mail: nrccte@louisville.edu
website: www.nrccte.org

The NRCCTE is committed to providing evidence-based solutions to the most vexing problems confronting career and technical education today, including how to better engage students in the school experience; how to improve academic as well as technical achievement; and how to improve the transition of college- and career-ready young people from high school to continuing education beyond high school. The NRCCTE is funded by the Office of Vocational and Adult Education of the US Department of Education. Its website offers research papers and brochures, podcasts, videos and webinars, as well as "Practitioner Wisdom Practices" and "Promising Practices," which are collections of instructional tips from teachers.

BIBLIOGRAPHY

Books

Rita Almeida, *The Right Skills for the Job? Rethinking Training Policies for Workers.* Washington, DC: World Bank, 2012.

Rachel Brooks, *Transitions from Education to Work: New Perspectives from Europe and Beyond.* New York: Palgrave Macmillan, 2009.

Gerald Chertavian, *A Year Up: How a Pioneering Program Teaches Young Adults Real Skills for Real Jobs—with Real Success.* New York: Viking, 2012.

David T. Conley, *College and Career Ready: Helping All Students Succeed Beyond High School.* San Francisco: Jossey-Bass, 2012.

Matthew B. Crawford, *Shop Class as Soulcraft: An Inquiry into the Value of Work.* New York: Penguin, 2010.

Linda Darling-Hammond, *The Flat World and Education: How America's Commitment to Equity Will Determine Our Future.* New York: Teachers College Press, 2011.

Kenneth C. Gray, *Getting Real: Helping Teens Find Their Future.* Thousand Oaks, CA: Corwin, 2009.

Chad Hanson, *The Community College and the Good Society: How the Liberal Arts Were Undermined and What We Can Do to Bring Them Back.* New Brunswick, NJ: Transaction, 2010.

Nancy Hoffman, *Schooling in the Workplace: How Six of the World's Best Vocational Education Systems Prepare Young People for Jobs and Life.* Cambridge, MA: Harvard Education Press, 2011.

Nancy Hoffman and Joel Vargas, *Minding the Gap: Why Integrating High School with College Makes Sense and How to Do It.* Cambridge, MA: Harvard Education Press, 2007.

Linda Murray, *Diploma Matters: A Field Guide for College and Career Readiness.* San Francisco: Jossey-Bass, 2011.

Richard Pring, *Education for All: The Future of Education and Training for 14–19 Year Olds.* New York: Routledge, 2009.

Diane Ravitch, *The Death and Life of the Great American School System: How Testing and Choice Are Undermining Education.* New York: Basic, 2011.

Andrew S. Rosen, *Change.edu: Rebooting for the New Talent Economy.* New York: Kaplan, 2011.

James R. Stone and Morgan V. Lewis, *College and Career Ready in the 21st Century: Making High School Matter.* New York: Teachers College Press, 2012.

Periodicals

Greg Beato, "Grade Inflation: The More We Spend on Higher Education, the More We Spend on Higher Education," *Reason*, February 2011.

Julia Belluz, "Hire Education: The Push to Make Grads More Job-Ready May Be Killing the Liberal Arts Tradition," *Maclean's*, November 22, 2010.

Dan Berrett, "Habits of Mind: Lessons for the Long Term," *Chronicle of Higher Education*, October 8, 2012.

Goldie Blumenstyk, "Meet the New For-Profit: The Low-Profit," *Chronicle of Higher Education*, October 14, 2012.

Kevin Carey, "America's Best Community Colleges: What Fifty Little-Known Two-Year Schools Can Teach the Rest of American Higher Education," *Washington Monthly*, September–October 2010.

Erin Carlyle, "Shakespeare with Power Tools: How a Humble Trade School Became the Best Community College in America," *Washington Monthly*, September–October 2010.

Kim Clark, "The Great Recession's Toll on Higher Education," *U.S. News & World Report*, September 10, 2010.

Gail Collins, "Reading, 'Riting and Revenues," *New York Times*, May 12, 2011.

Tyler Cowan, "Graduates' Pay Is Slipping, but Still Outpaces Others," *New York Times*, March 2, 2012.

Economist, "Too Narrow, Too Soon? Vocational Training," June 19, 2010.

Rana Foroohar, "These Schools Mean Business," *Time*, April 9, 2012.

Catherine Gewertz, "Advocates Press for New Definition of Career Readiness," *Education Week*, April 21, 2010.

Joe Klein, "Learning That Works," *Time*, May 14, 2012.

Lee Lawrence, "Bachelor's Degree: Has It Lost Its Edge and Its Value?," *Christian Science Monitor*, June 17, 2012.

Bill Maxwell, "Community Colleges Need to Cast Wider Net," *Tampa Bay (FL) Times*, March 18, 2012.

David Moltz, "Crunch Time for 2-Year Colleges," *Inside Higher Ed*, March 11, 2010.

David Mulry, "Why I Gave up Teaching at a Community College," *Chronicle of Higher Education*, April 18, 2010.

Hollister K. Petraeus, "For-Profit Colleges, Vulnerable G.I.'s," *New York Times*, September 22, 2011.

Jane S. Shaw, "The Future Is For-Profit: Education Entrepreneurs Are Poised to Upset the Complacent Higher-Ed Establishment," *National Review*, October 5, 2009.

Burck Smith, "Let's Deregulate Online Learning," *Chronicle of Higher Education*, November 6, 2011.

USA Today, "In Today's Economy, Age 16 Is Too Soon to Drop Out of School," February 15, 2012.

Adam Weinstein, "Let's Enroll!," *Mother Jones*, September–October 2011.

Mary Ann Zehr, "Latino Students Less Likely to Select Four-Year Colleges: Finances and Poor Counseling Among Reasons Cited," *Education Week*, August 11, 2010.

A

AAC&U (Association of American Colleges and Universities), 25, 38
Allen, Paul, 75
Altucher, James, 71–72, 73
American Community Survey (US Census Bureau), 17
American Graduation Initiative, 90, 92–97
American Public University, 87
Associate's degree/certificate
  percentage of first-time, full-time students earning within three years, 84
  percentage of institutions offering, by type, 34
Association of American Colleges and Universities (AAC&U), 25, 38

B

Baum, Sandy, 17, 18, 20, 22
Bennett, Antoine, 81
Biden, Jill, 94
Brookings Institution, 17, 18, 22
Brynjolfsson, Erik, 66
Bureau of Labor Statistics, 74
Bureau of Labor Statistics, US, 5

Butrymowicz, Sarah, 42

C

Callan, Patrick M., 64
Career academies, 27
Career and technical education (CTE)
  California graduates in, 45
  can get dropouts back on track, 77–82
  completion rates in, 27–28
  federal support for, by year, 56
  in high school takes time away from other studies, 42–49
  must do better job at preparing students for college, 50–57
  prepares students for college/careers, 9–15
  purpose of, 7
Career technical student organizations (CTSOs), 13
Carey, Kevin, 83
Carl D. Perkins Career and Technical Education Act (2006), 55, 105
Carnevale, Anthony P., 21, 30, 46
Census Bureau, US, 17

Center on Education and the Workforce (Georgetown University), 21, 24, 27

Certificate programs, lead to well-paying jobs, 30–35

Certificates, postsecondary
lead to well-paying jobs, 30–35
percentage of institutions awarding, by type, 34

Chronicle of Higher Education (journal), 73

Chrysler, Walter P., 101

Civil Rights Project (University of California, Los Angeles), 63

Clifford, Michael, 83, 85–86

Cohen, Mark, 82

College degrees
are best career preparation, 16–22
are not worth the cost, 70–76
percentage of adults holding, 47
percentage of population holding, 96
postsecondary certificates as stepping stones toward, 31

College/higher education
for all, is misguided concept, 65–69
escalating tuition in, 61–62
for-profit, is expensive but effective, 83–89
low-income/minority students are being squeezed out of, 58–64

College loans/debt, 23–24, 73–74
has overtaken US credit-card debt, 72

Community colleges
cascade effect and, 60–61
disconnect between programs offered by, 68
federal government should increase support for, 90–97
percentage of high-income students choosing, 61
prevalence of low-income students in, 63

Complete College America, 28

Conference Board, 25

ConnectEd, 49

CTE. *See* Career and technical education

D

Dell, Michael, 75

DeMause, Neil, 16

Department of Education, US, 44

Department of Labor, US, 25

Dropout rate, trend in, 79

Duncan, Arne, 26, 50, 53, 104

E

Earnings
of career academy graduates, 27

of college *vs.* high-school graduates, 73–74

for full-time workers with college degrees *vs.* high school diplomas, 22

life-time, impact of four-year degree on, 17

median weekly, by educational level, *19*

of recent graduates/ experienced workers, by field of study, *75*

working-class, impact of decline in unions on, 66–67

Economic Policy Institute (EPI), 18, 21

Educational level, unemployment rate/earnings by, *19*

Elementary and Secondary Education Act (1965), 26

Ellison, Larry, 75

Employer surveys, 39

  on essential learning outcomes, *38*

  on high need for training programs, by job skill, *14*

  on preparation of recent graduates, 25

EPI (Economic Policy Institute), 18, 21

F

Federal government

  history of funding of vocational education by, 26

should increase support for community colleges, 90–97

spending on CTE by, by year, *56*

will condition CTE funding on improved student outcomes, 54–55

Forbes (magazine), 66

Ford, Henry, 101

Four-year degrees. *See* College degrees

G

Gates, Bill, 75

Geffen, David, 76

Georgetown University, 21, 24, 27

Germany, career-focused education system of, 98–103

GI Bill, 92

Goldstein, Dana, 104

Gossett, Barry, 76

Graduation rates, high school, 44

Grand Canyon University, 85, 88

Granholm, Jennifer, 93

Gray, Kenneth, 44

Great Recession, 54

  unemployment rates in, 5

Green, Kimberly, 45, 46

Greenstone, Michael, 22

H

Hamilton Project (Brookings Institution), 17, 18

Hanson, Andrew R., 30
Harkin, Tom, 89
High school students, should have more opportunities for workplace experience, 105–110
High School Survey of Student Engagement, 25–26
Himelstein, Scott, 47
Hoachlander, Gary, 49
Hoffman, Nancy, 105

J
Job training, today's workers need more than, 36–41
Jobs
  percentages of/workers qualified for, by skill level, 25
  projection of educational requirements for, 24
Jobs, Steve, 75

K
Kaplan University, 87
Kaufman, Sarah, 70
Kelly, Andrew P., 23
Klein, Ezra, 23–24
Kulman, Kellie, 91

L
Labor unions, 102
  decline of, 66–67
Land grant colleges, 92
Liberal education
  as class-based, 107

importance of, 36–41
Liberal Education and America's Promise (LEAP) initiative (Association of American Colleges and Universities), 38
Lincoln, Abraham, 92
Lotterman, Edward, 98
Low-income students, are being squeezed out of higher education, 58–64

M
Manufacturing Institute, 5–6
McAfee, Andrew, 66
Miller, Harris, 86
Minority students, are being squeezed out of higher education, 58–64
Mishel, Lawrence, 18, 21

N
Nation (magazine), 105
National Association of State Directors of Career Technical Education Consortium, 9, 44–45
National Career Clusters, 13
National Center on Education and the Economy, 69
National Student Clearinghouse (NSC), 60
New York Times (newspaper), 68
NSC (National Student Clearinghouse), 60

Nunn, Sam, 84

O
Obama, Barack/Obama administration, 26, 82, 90, 93
  on federal aid to for-profit colleges, 85
  on need for postsecondary career training, 54
  vocational education plan of, 105
Occupy Wall Street protests, 23
Opinion polls. *See* Employer surveys; Surveys

P
Pell Grants, 85, 92
Polls. *See* Employer surveys; Surveys
Pratt, Steven, 38–39

R
Race Against the Machine (Brynjolfsson and McAfee), 66
Reilly, Kevin P., 6–7
Rhoades, Gary, 58
Roosevelt, Franklin D., 92
Rose, Stephen J., 30
Rutgers Center for Workforce Development, 17

S
Salazar, Sid, 43

Santorum, Rick, 65–66, *67*
Schooling in the Workplace (Hoffman), 105
Shrimp, Fran, 46, 47
Snyder, Daniel, 76
Spilde, Mary, 36
Steenhausen, Paul, 59
Stone, James R., 65
Stoneman, Dorothy, 77
Student loans. *See* College loans/debt
Surveys
  of high-school students on relevance of curriculum, 25–26
  of small business CEOs on skills gap, *102*
  See also Employer surveys
Switzerland, transitional education in, 106, 107–110

T
Tough Choices, Tough Times (National Center on Education and the Economy), 69

U
Unemployment/ unemployment rate
  among college graduates, 74
  by educational level, *19*
  Germany's career-focused education system reduces, 98–103
  in Great Recession, 5
  youth, 105

University of California, Los Angeles, 63
University of Phoenix, 87
Up to the Challenge, 7

V
Vauclain, Samuel, 101
Vedder, Richard, 73, 74
Vocational programs, are good investments, 23–29
Volkswagen, 107

W
Wal-Mart, 87

Wall Street Journal (newspaper), 72
Welch, Jack, 85–86
Workplace experience, high school students should have more opportunities for, 105–110

Y
YouthBuild program, 77–82, 80

Z
Zuckerberg, Mark, 20

PICTURE CREDITS